the *Big Book* of *Decorative Borders*

JODIE BUSHMAN

NORTH LIGHT BOOKS
CINCINNATI, OHIO
www.artistsnetwork.com

About the Author

Jodie Bushman's painting career began in 1970 with an art course at a local college. She has been painting ever since. The borders and embellishments in this book are the culmination of those many years of design creativity. Jodie is an Associate Designer for Delta paints, and her artwork has been published in several popular painting magazines. When she is not teaching at seminars and conventions across the country, Jodie can be found at her own Rainshadow Studio at the base of beautiful Mt. Hood in Oregon, where she lives with her husband, John.

metric conversion chart

TO CONVERT	TO	MULTIPLY BY
Inches	Centimeters	2.54
Centimeters	Inches	0.4
Feet	Centimeters	30.5
Centimeters	Feet	0.03
Yards	Meters	0.9
Meters	Yards	1.1
Sq. Inches	Sq. Centimeters	6.45
Sq. Centimeters	Sq. Inches	0.16
Sq. Feet	Sq. Meters	0.09
Sq. Meters	Sq. Feet	10.8
Sq. Yards	Sq. Meters	0.8
Sq. Meters	Sq. Yards	1.2
Pounds	Kilograms	0.45
Kilograms	Pounds	2.2
Ounces	Grams	28.4
Grams	Ounces	0.04

Published by North Light Books, an imprint of F&W Publications, Inc., 4700 E. Galbraith Rd., Cincinnati, Ohio 45236. (800) 289-0963. First edition.

Other fine North Light Books are available from your local bookstore, art supply store or directly from the publisher.

07 06 05 04   5 4 3

Library of Congress Cataloging-in-Publication Data

Bushman, Jodie
The big book of decorative borders / Jodie Bushman.
  p. cm.
Includes index.
ISBN 1-58180-335-4 (pbk. : alk. paper) -- ISBN 1-58180-336-2 (alk. paper)
1. Painting--Technique. 2. Decoration and ornament. 3. Borders, Ornamental (Decorative arts) I. Title.

TT385.B873 2003

2003044194

Editor: Kathy Kipp
Production Coordinator: Kristen Heller
Designer: Joanna Detz
Layout Artist: Kathy Gardner
Photographer: Christine Polomsky

Acknowledgments

I would like to thank JoSonja Jansen, whose lessons
in traditional decorative painting taught us that we
are all artists and don't let anyone tell you anything
different! Thanks also to Donna Santos and the
"Friday Class" ladies.

I am grateful to the late Pat Peniston, who many
years ago taught me the easy and logical rose painting
method you'll see on pages 64-65 of this book. Her
book, *Roses from Pat* (1979), is out of print but
look for it at your library or used book store.

Mostly, a big thank you to my editor Kathy Kipp,
my new best friend at North Light Books, for her
laughter, enthusiasm and encouragement, and to
photographer Christine Polomsky for making
the photo shoot fun!

Dedication

*I dedicate this book to my late mother and big
sister. One called me a "toe" painter (tole
painter) and the other called me a "troll"
painter. Also, to my family—husband John,
and daughters Angela, Mary Ann, Lisa and
Tricia—who for many years tolerated my out-
of-town trips and instant dinners.*

Table of Contents

Introduction

After teaching painting for many years, and seeing so many painted projects that were beautiful but seemed to be lacking something, I realized there was a need for a large reference book of borders and embellishments that artists could use to finish off their work and provide a visual frame.

The borders in this book are meant to fill that need, and may be copied right out of the book and applied to your own work. There are hundreds to choose from and they range from simple to very ornate, from cute and whimsical to classically beautiful.

As you'll see in this book, borders can be used anywhere, on projects of any size and shape. They can even be used on walls and around windows and doors. Project 10, the Daisy Wall Border, shows you how to use the same basic design around an oval picture frame and around the window frame in a young girl's bedroom.

Use your imagination and you'll find many places to add borders, including stationery, greeting cards, scrapbooks and photo albums, flower pots, a matching set of dishes and tableware, picture frames, tabletops, home decorating accessories, wall and ceiling borders, and so much more. Use your favorite colors and make these borders your own. Have fun!

Jodie Bushman

Materials Needed

Most of the supplies you will need to paint borders and embellishments can be found at your local art and craft supply store and home improvement center. The brushes I used to paint the borders in this book are made by Loew-Cornell, and the acrylic paints are by Delta (see the Resources on page 142 for addresses). You may use whichever brands you are comfortable with; however, painting borders is much easier if you use the best quality brushes and paints you can afford.

The photo at right shows all of the supplies I used for the projects in this book. You may already have many of these items on hand, such as pencils, sanding pads and tracing paper. The rest are inexpensive and can be found at your local stores.

My palette is just a plastic box I found in the school supplies section of my local store. I put a dampened shop towel in between the folds of a piece of deli wrap to keep my paints moist. When I'm finished painting for the day, I just remoisten the shop towel and close the lid—my paints stay fresh for the next day.

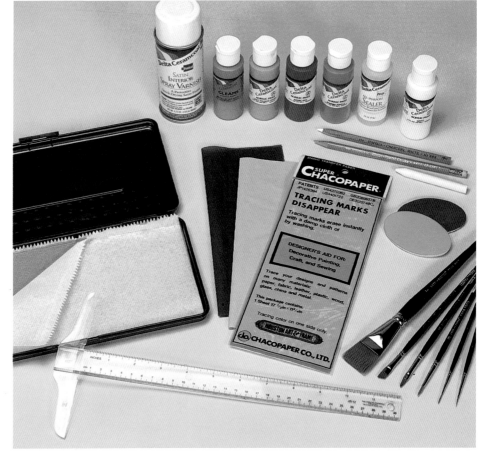

Shown here are the supplies I used to paint the projects in this book. The brushes are all by Loew-Cornell and include: series 7350 18/0 liner, 10/0 liner, no. 0 liner; a series 7400 ¼-inch (6mm) angular; a series 7500 no. 6 filbert; a series 7000 no. 3 round; and a 1-inch (25mm) wide prep brush (mine is an old, used brush I keep on hand for prep work such as basecoating). The paints are Delta Ceramcoat bottled acrylics, and the gold paint is Delta Gleams 14K Gold. Other supplies you'll need include regular lead pencils, white and gray chalk pencils, school chalk, tracing paper, gray and black graphite paper, a stylus, blue Super Chacopaper, sanding pad, wood sealer, interior spray varnish, and a 1-inch (25mm) wide T-square ruler.

How to Make a Wet Palette

1 You'll need a piece of deli wrap paper (available from your local supermarket), a piece of blue shop towel (available at a home center or hardware store), and a plastic pencil box with a hinged lid (available from a discount store).

2 Unfold the deli wrap paper and lay half of it on the bottom of the pencil box. Place the blue shop towel over the deli paper and pour water over the shop towel to dampen.

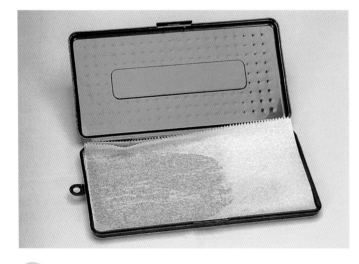

3 Then fold the other half of the deli wrap over the wet shop towel and smooth it down.

4 If you need to redampen the shop towel, just pull back one corner of the deli wrap and add a little more water.

Loading the Brush with Paint

5 To load a liner brush or any other round brush, dip it into the paint puddle, then roll and pull the brush out of the puddle. This will maintain the point of the brush and allow you to have an even, full load of paint.

6 When loading an angular brush, a filbert or a flat brush, start with one side of the brush. Dip into the puddle and pull out.

7 Flip the brush over, and dip and pull the other side. Blend on the palette.

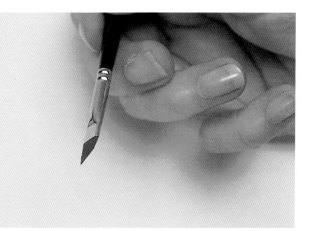

8 This will allow even loading across the brush and prevent ridges when you paint.

9 This is what happens if the brush isn't properly loaded—you get ridges and uneven blobs of paint!

10 To double load a flat, angular or filbert brush, dip one corner of the brush into the first color.

11 Dip the other corner into the second color.

12 Blend the two colors on your palette.

13 To sideload a brush, dampen it with water, then pull one side of the dampened brush through the side of the paint puddle. Leave the other side free of paint. Blend on the palette.

How to Make Dots of All Sizes

14 To make dots easily, just use the tip end of your brush handle. Dip it into your paint puddle.

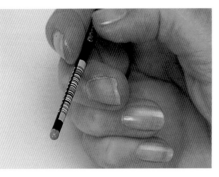

15 This is how much paint you should have on the tip end of your brush handle.

16 To make uniformly sized dots, re-load your brush handle with paint every time you make a dot.

17 To make smaller, even tiny dots, use a stylus with two different-sized ball ends. Dip one end into the paint.

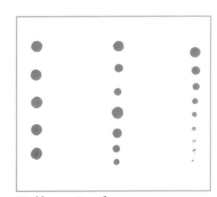

Uniform, Random and Diminishing Dots
(Left) Make uniformly sized dots by reloading the tip end of your brush handle every time. (Middle) Make randomly sized dots by reloading every third or fourth dot. (Right) Make diminishing dots by not reloading and by touching the surface until the paint runs out.

Dots Made with a Stylus
Here are uniform, random, and diminishing dots made with the ball ends of a stylus.

SEALING AND SANDING

18 Seal your raw wooden surfaces by brushing on wood sealer with a large flat brush. Let it dry thoroughly.

19 Sand the sealed surface with a fine grit sanding pad to smooth it. Remove all the sanding dust with a tack cloth or a dampened shop towel.

BASECOATING AND FINISHING

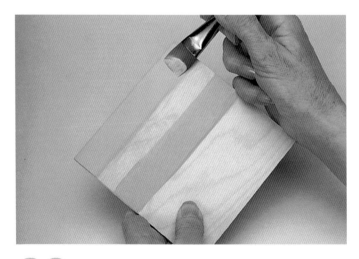

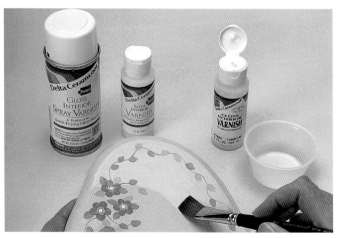

20 Apply your basecoat with a large flat brush, going with the grain of the wood. You will almost always need to apply a second coat after the first one has dried. Only one coat allows the grain of the wood to show through, as you can see in the lower stripe of paint above. Sand lightly between coats. If you're going to be doing fine linework, sand lightly one final time before you begin to paint to give the basecoated surface as much smoothness as possible.

21 After your painted design is finished and completely dry, make sure you remove any leftover tracing lines. If you transferred your pattern with blue Super Chacopaper, just wipe it off with a damp paper towel. If you used graphite paper, erase the lines with a white plastic eraser. To protect your painting, use either a spray-on or brush-on acrylic varnish. But first, be sure to sign your work—be proud of what you've done!

Building a Border

The Elements of a Border

All borders, from the simplest to the most intricate, have certain elements in common. These elements make building a border easy, straightforward and logical, no matter what shape your border is—rectangular, round, oval or square. These elements include the:
- Guideline: the centerline of the design.
- Boundary Lines: the outermost edges of the design. Also called "helper lines."
- Spine: the line that the border is built upon, for example, a "C" or "S" shape.

In the photos below and on the facing page, you will see how to begin creating simple borders using these three elements.

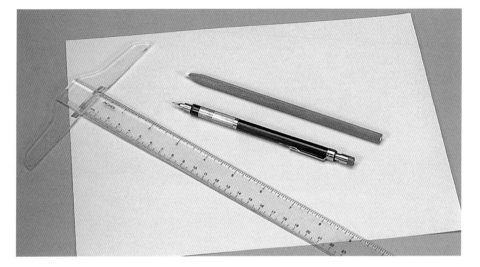

1 First, gather together a few drawing materials: a 1-inch (25mm) wide, see-through plastic T-square ruler; a mechanical pencil; a chalk pencil; and a piece of paper.

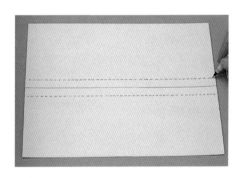

2 Draw a solid horizontal line across the center of your paper using your ruler and pencil. This is your Guideline. (In these photos, I'm using a black, fine point marker pen only so you can see the lines more easily.) Then on both sides of the Guideline, add dashed or broken lines. These are your Boundary, or helper, lines. They will be the outer edges of your border and will help contain the border design area within even lines.

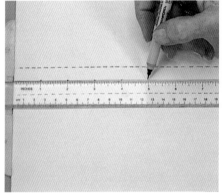

3 Along the solid Guideline, mark off evenly spaced dots. These are called "section dots." They help you keep each section of your border design the same size.

4 Next, add a series of small "helper dots" near the larger section dots. Here, I placed the helper dots ¼ inch (6mm) to the right of each section dot. These helper dots are the starting points for the curving lines called "S" strokes that you'll see on the next page.

Regular and Elongated S-stroke Spine

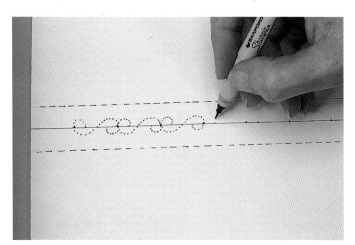

5 Between each section dot in this photo, you will see an "S" shaped series of dots. This S-shape is the "Spine." It travels above and below the center Guideline. Begin the S-stroke spine on the first helper dot at the left. Curve your line up and over to the first section dot at the left. Then come down below the Guideline and make an S-shaped curve up and over to the next large section dot. Cross the Guideline again, curving downward and to the left. Repeat this as often as desired, always starting on the helper dot.

To make the elongated S-stroke spine shown below, just stretch out the curving line to two section dots rather than one. Again, start on the helper dot and curve up and over to the section dot at the left.

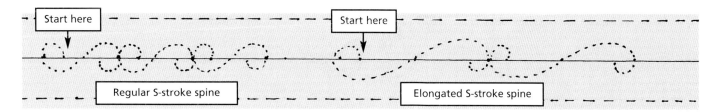

Start here

Start here

Regular S-stroke spine

Elongated S-stroke spine

C-stroke Spine

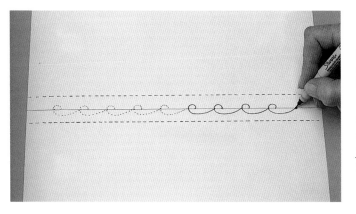

6 To make a C-stroke spine, begin as shown in steps 2, 3 and 4 on the facing page. Draw a solid line for your center Guideline, and dashed lines for the Boundary Lines. Place large section dots 1 inch (25mm) apart along the Guideline, then add helper dots ¼-inch (6mm) to the right of each section dot.

Start your C-stroke spine on the first helper dot at the left. Curve up and over to the left to the large section dot. Curve down, then come back up and connect to the next section dot at the right. Start your next C-stroke at the helper dot to the right of where you just finished. To see the effect, draw a solid line over your dotted line.

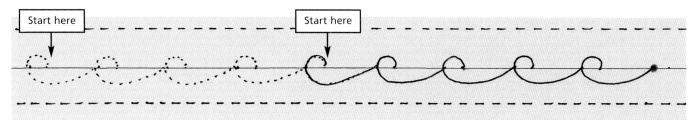

Start here

Start here

Scroll Spine

A scroll spine can be made from the C-stroke spine. Simply have one C-stroke curve under the center guideline, and the next one curve over it. Again, start your stroke on the helper dot and slide off the back of the previous scroll.

Lifeline Spine

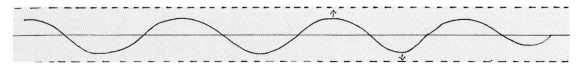

A lifeline is a spine that is more free-flowing between the two boundary, or helper, lines.

C-stroke Scroll with Hooks

To make a slightly more elaborate border, start with a scroll spine and add little "hook" strokes (the red arrows above indicate the hook strokes). Here I've drawn the C-strokes slightly away from the section dots so you can more easily see where they are.

C-stroke Spine with Comma Strokes

You can also embellish your basic C-stroke spine with three little comma strokes as shown on the left half above. On the right half is a variation on that theme: two comma strokes and one hook stroke. Again, I've drawn the C-strokes slightly away from the section dots so you can see them more easily.

S-stroke Spine with Commas & Hooks

You can embellish a basic S-stroke spine with two little S-stroke leaves on each side, as shown on the left half above. Then add large hook strokes above and below each end of the S-stroke, as shown on the right half above.

C-stroke Scroll with Hooks and Crosshatching

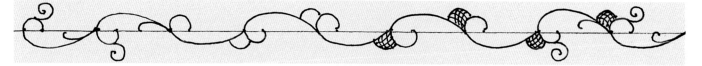

This is a C-stroke spine embellished with hook strokes and little fan shapes that are then filled in with crosshatching.

S-stroke Spine with Hooks, Commas, Dots & Flowers

Now we're getting really fancy! This is a basic S-stroke spine that is embellished with large hook strokes, little S-stroke leaves and little comma stroke leaves, diminishing dots, and even a five-petal "flower" in the center of each of the two sections on the right. As you can see, it's easy to "build" an elaborate-looking border from a selection of very simple strokes. Just choose your favorites!

BOUNDARY LINES

The two outside boundary lines—those dashed lines you saw on pages 12-14—can be embellished just like the spines can. The three examples below show upper and lower boundary lines drawn with simple yet effective strokes. The first one has a series of connecting scallops with tiny circle dots. The second has a dot-dash design. And the third is simply a wavy line.

At right is a selection of boundary lines in different colors. Pick out some you like and place tracing paper over the page to practice making the strokes. After a while you will get into the rhythm of each design and it will go very quickly. Draw helper lines and dots on your tracing paper to help keep your spacing consistent. This is the secret to professional-looking borders.

Boundary Lines in Color

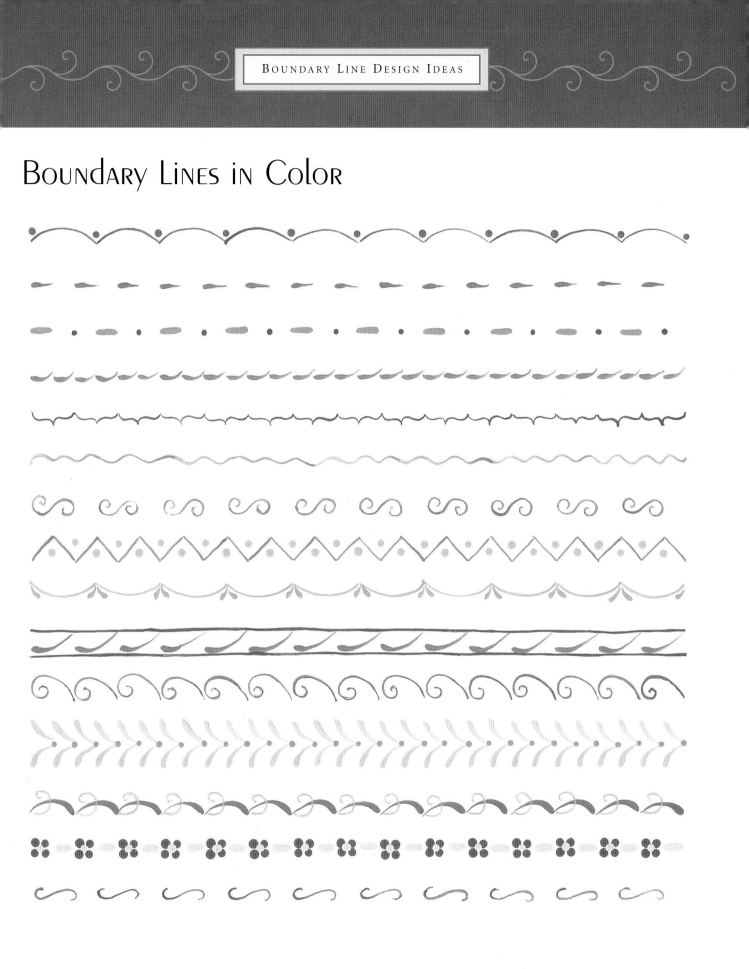

CANVAS PICTURE FRAME

Project One

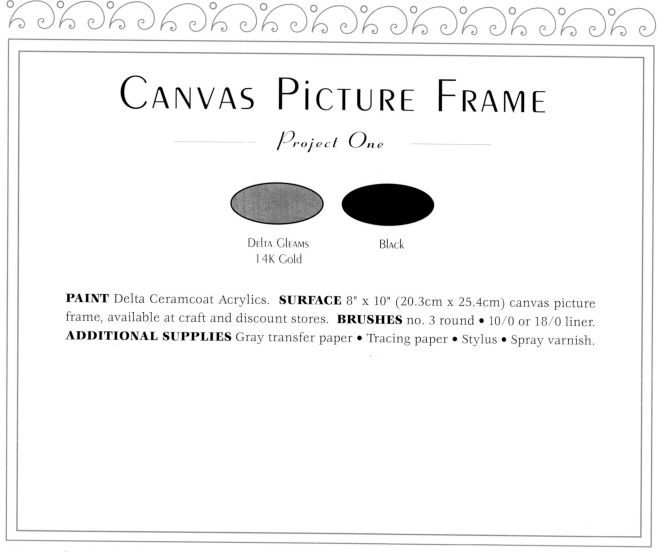

Delta Gleams
14K Gold

Black

PAINT Delta Ceramcoat Acrylics. **SURFACE** 8" x 10" (20.3cm x 25.4cm) canvas picture frame, available at craft and discount stores. **BRUSHES** no. 3 round • 10/0 or 18/0 liner.
ADDITIONAL SUPPLIES Gray transfer paper • Tracing paper • Stylus • Spray varnish.

1 Basecoat the canvas frame with two to three coats of gold acrylic paint. Let each coat dry before applying the next. Paint the inner edge of the center opening with Black. Let dry.

2 Trace the pattern (see next page) onto the frame with a piece of gray transfer paper and a stylus.

Outer and Inner Borders

3 Load a liner brush with Black. Paint large, connecting C-strokes along the outer edges of all four sides, stopping short of the corners. Along the inside edge, paint simple scallops that are evenly spaced.

4 Paint a design of three comma strokes in each outer corner.

This pattern may be hand-traced or photocopied for personal use only. Enlarge at 167 percent to bring it up to full size. The dotted line is the halfway point of the design, which is a mirror image top to bottom. Trace the top half of the pattern onto your frame, then flip the pattern over to trace the bottom half.

Embellishments

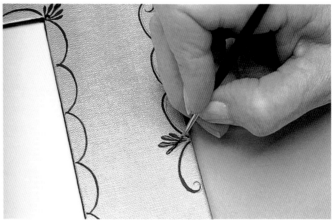

5 Dip the tip end of your brush handle into the puddle of Black paint and add three dots of diminishing size along the outer edges of the frame's long side. See the photo below for placement.

6 At the middle of the outer edges, add a fan-shaped cluster of five comma strokes. Do the same at the inner corners, then place a dot at the base where the comma tails meet to tidy them up. Allow all the paint to dry completely. Remove the transfer lines, then finish with a spray gloss varnish.

Completed Frame

Recep[tion]
immediately follo[wing]
Baur's Oper[a]
625 South Fi[...]
Springfield, [...]

Mini Photo Album

Project Two

14K Gold

PAINT Delta PermEnamel. **SURFACE** Mini photo album with white vinyl cover, available at craft and discount stores. This one came with a gold border already imprinted on the cover and spine. **BRUSHES** no. 0 liner • ¼-inch (6mm) angular • an old, used brush for applying the gloss glaze. **ADDITIONAL SUPPLIES** Delta PermEnamel Surface Cleaner & Conditioner • Delta Air-Dry PermEnamel Thinner/Diluent • Delta Clear Gloss Glaze • Tracing paper and stylus • Blue Super Chacopaper • Script lettering stencil (optional).

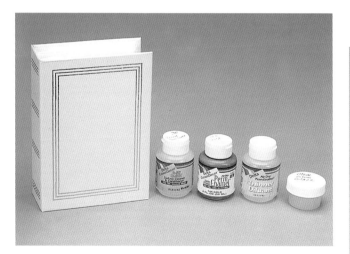

1 Assemble your materials. I prefer to pour a small amount of the Clear Gloss Glaze into another small container and keep the original container tightly closed.

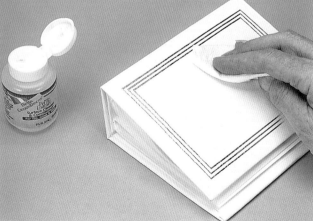

2 Before you begin painting, wipe the vinyl cover with the cleaner/conditioner and a plain white paper towel.

These patterns may be hand-traced or
photocopied for personal use only.
They are shown here full size.

3 Transfer the pattern using blue Super Chacopaper and a stylus. It may be easier to tape the pattern down once you have it centered. Notice that the design is a mirror image of itself top to bottom and left to right. If you divide the pattern in half and then into fourths, you'll see that each quadrant is exactly the same design.

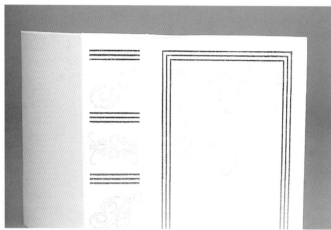

4 This is how the pattern looks after being transferred onto the photo album cover and spine. Because this design is the same in all four quadrants, I transferred only part of the pattern to save time. In this photo you can see the entire top left quadrant and part of the top right.

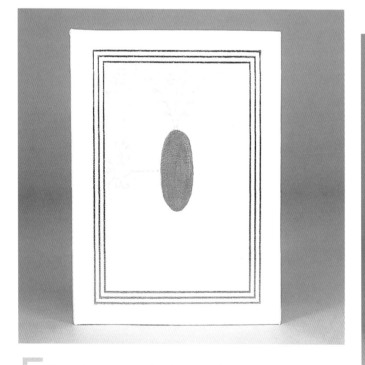

5 Paint the center oval with two to three coats of 14K Gold on a ¼-inch (6mm) angular brush. Let dry between coats.

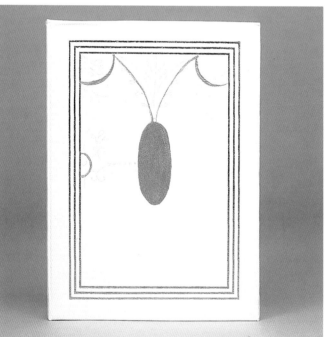

6 Load a no. 0 liner with 14K Gold and paint the corner bands and the main lines of the design. If the paint needs to be thinned for the linework, use the thinner/diluent, not water.

Add Embellishments

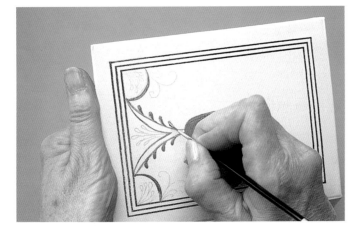

7 Add the secondary lines and four little comma strokes on each side of the "V"-shaped lines. Turn the album so you are pulling the comma strokes into the lines.

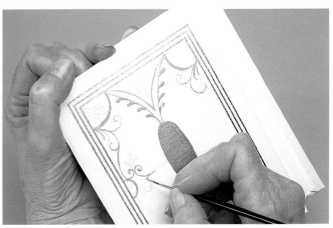

8 Paint scrolls coming out from the corners and connecting to the midway scrolls. Paint the scrolls that form the "pocket" for the crosshatching.

9 In the corners and the middle of the top, paint five long comma strokes in a fan shape. On the scrolls, add three shorter comma strokes.

10 Paint the crosshatching in the "pockets" you painted in Step 8. Then dip the tip end of your brush handle into the Gold paint and add dots as shown. Complete the other portions of the front cover using the same strokes.

Complete the Cover and Paint the Spine

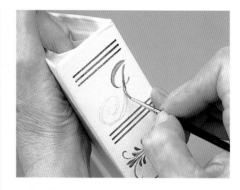

11 On the spine, the design in the middle is a combination of hook strokes and commas. Start with the four hook strokes and the center dot.

12 Fill in with sixteen short comma strokes radiating out from the center dot. Note that the center commas are much more curved than the side ones.

13 Paint your choice of lettering above and below the design with 14K Gold on the no. 0 liner. Let dry and add a second coat. (There are many styles of lettering stencils at your local craft store from which you can trace your own initials.)

Allow to dry thoroughly. Using a damp paper towel, gently remove the blue transfer lines. The gold paint is still very tender, so protect it with a coat of Clear Gloss Glaze. Let dry.

Completed
Front Cover

Completed
Spine

Pink Oval Tray

Project Three

Rose Petal Pink Pink Quartz Hydrangea Pink White

PAINT Delta Ceramcoat Acrylics. **SURFACE** Oval wooden tray, 9" x 15" (22.9cm x 38.1cm), available at craft supply stores. **BRUSHES** ¼-inch (6mm) angular • no. 3 round • 18/0 liner. **ADDITIONAL SUPPLIES** Wood sealer • Sanding pad • Tack cloth • Tracing paper • Stylus • Gray chalk pencil • T-square ruler • Satin varnish.

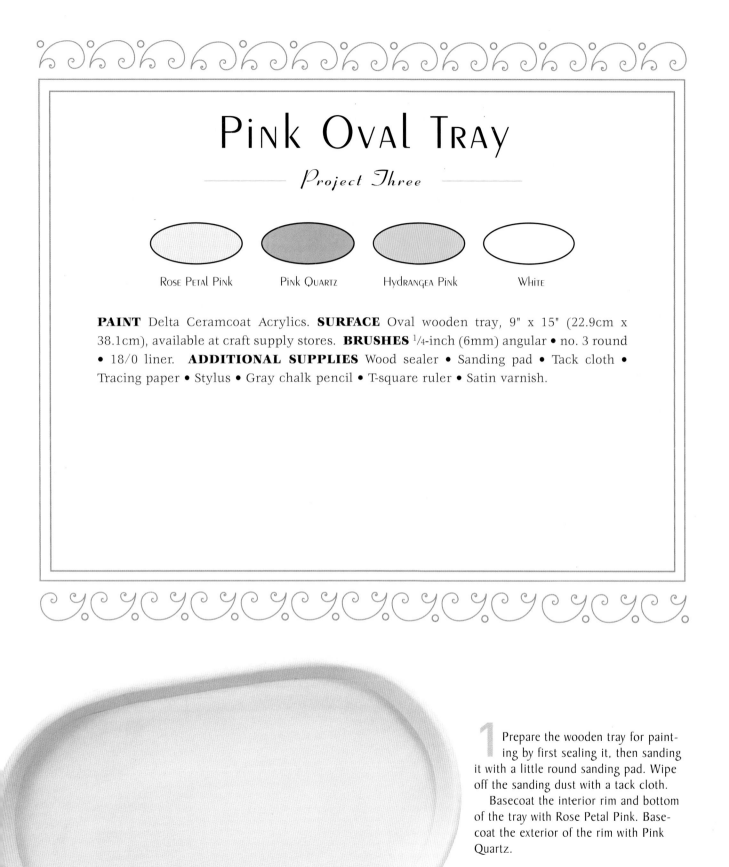

1 Prepare the wooden tray for painting by first sealing it, then sanding it with a little round sanding pad. Wipe off the sanding dust with a tack cloth.

Basecoat the interior rim and bottom of the tray with Rose Petal Pink. Basecoat the exterior of the rim with Pink Quartz.

TRANSFER THE PATTERN

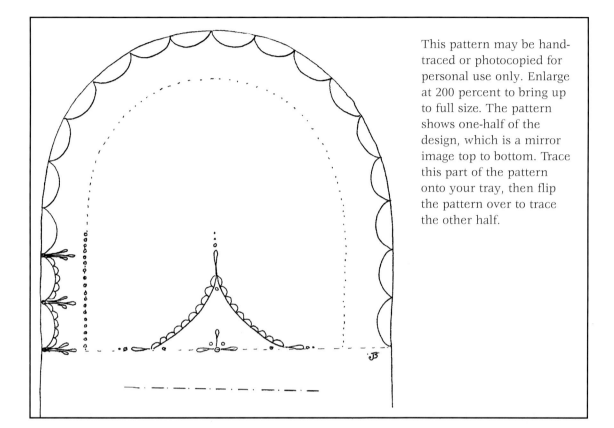

This pattern may be hand-traced or photocopied for personal use only. Enlarge at 200 percent to bring up to full size. The pattern shows one-half of the design, which is a mirror image top to bottom. Trace this part of the pattern onto your tray, then flip the pattern over to trace the other half.

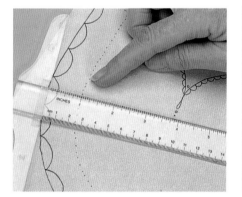

2 Referring to the pattern, notice that there are scallops at 1-inch (25mm) intervals that curve out to about ¹⁄4 inch (6mm) all around the inside of the tray bottom.

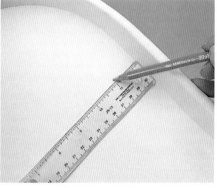

3 With a gray chalk pencil and a ruler, mark 1-inch (25mm) intervals around the perimeter of the tray bottom. Then in the middle of each interval, make a mark ¹⁄4 inch (6mm) out from the side of the rim.

4 Draw a curved scallop line from between the two 1-inch (25mm) marks, going through the ¹⁄4-inch (6mm) mark. Measure out 1 inch (25mm) from the rim and mark a dotted boundary or helper line.

Paint the Center Motif

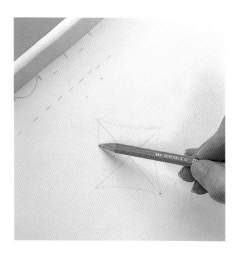

5 Measure the length and width of the tray bottom to determine your center point, and mark it with the gray chalk pencil. Draw 4 lines out in each direction 1½ inches (38mm) long. Connect the outer points with 4 slightly curved lines. This is your basic spine.

6 Base in the center motif with Hydrangea Pink on a ¼-inch (6mm) angular brush. Two coats may be necessary.

7 Sideload a ¼-inch (6mm) angular brush into Pink Quartz.

8 Shade the four curved sides of the center motif to help "lift" it from the background and give it some depth.

9 Using a small liner brush and slightly thinned Pink Quartz, paint the small lacy scallops freehand. With White on a no. 3 round, paint the 4 teardrops in the center. Radiating out from the four points, add a comma and 3 dots on the horizontal axis, and 2 dots on the other axis. Use the tip end of your brush handle dipped in White to make the dots.

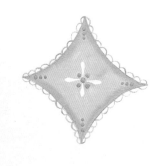

10 Now dip the brush handle end into Pink Quartz and add 4 small dots around the center and one larger dot dead center. Add 3 dots at each corner. The center motif is now complete.

11 For the scalloped edge around the perimeter of the tray bottom, base in the scallops with Hydrangea Pink on a ¼-inch (6mm) angular brush. Two coats may be needed. Sideload the ¼-inch (6mm) angular with Pink Quartz and shade along where the rim joins the tray bottom. Load a liner with slightly thinned Pink Quartz and freehand 5 small lacy loops along each scallop edge.

12 Load a no. 3 round with White and pull 3 strokes between each scallop. The middle stroke is the longest one, and it should be the same length all the way around the tray. Add Pink Quartz dots between each scallop at the base of the white strokes.

13 For the "pearl necklace" of white dots, it's important to reload White paint onto the tip end of your brush handle for each dot. Otherwise, your dots will diminish in size and ruin the uniform look.

14 Dot the white pearl necklace along the dashed helper line all the way around the tray bottom.

Completed Tray

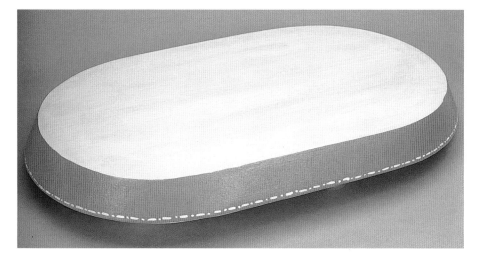

15 Turn the tray over and decorate the top edge of the outside rim with a dot-dash design in White. Allow to dry completely. With a damp paper towel, remove all chalk and transfer lines. Protect the tray with a satin varnish.

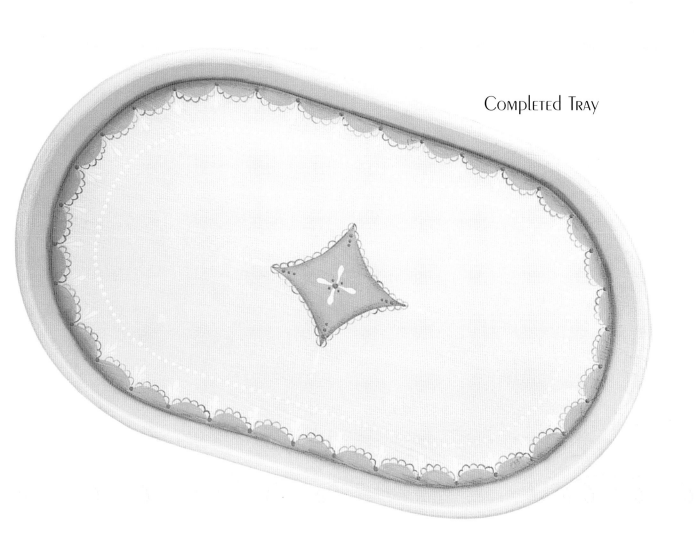

Completed Tray

Blue Heart Basket

Project Four

Coastline Blue	Green Sea	Silver Pine	Bahama Purple	Pale Yellow

PAINT Delta Ceramcoat Acrylics. **SURFACE** Wooden heart-shaped lid on a woven basket, from Stan Brown Arts & Crafts catalog. **BRUSHES** no. 4 filbert • no. 3 round • 18/0 liner. **ADDITIONAL SUPPLIES** Wood sealer • Sanding pad • Tack cloth • Tracing paper • Stylus • Blue Super Chacopaper • Satin varnish.

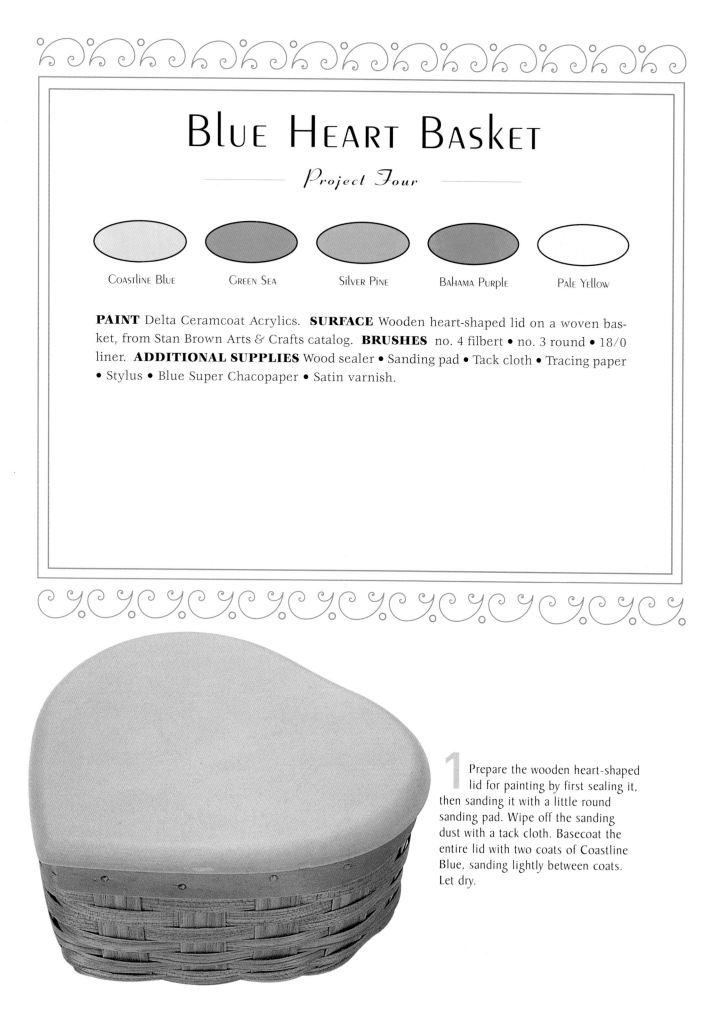

1 Prepare the wooden heart-shaped lid for painting by first sealing it, then sanding it with a little round sanding pad. Wipe off the sanding dust with a tack cloth. Basecoat the entire lid with two coats of Coastline Blue, sanding lightly between coats. Let dry.

Transfer the Pattern and Paint the Leaves

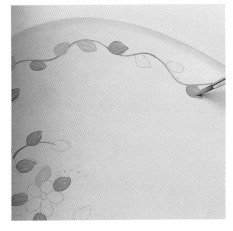

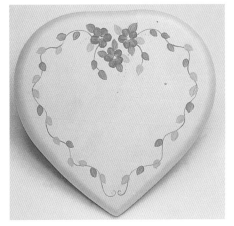

2 Transfer the pattern onto the base-coated lid. With Green Sea on a liner brush, paint the main vines (the lifeline) on both sides and the trailing stems at the top.

3 For the leaves, use two colors—Green Sea and Silver Pine. Place them randomly along the main vine and at the center top. Use a no. 3 round and make each leaf with two short strokes, bringing them to a point. Let dry.

4 Load a no. 4 filbert with Bahama Purple and paint the five-petal flowers at the top center of the lid.

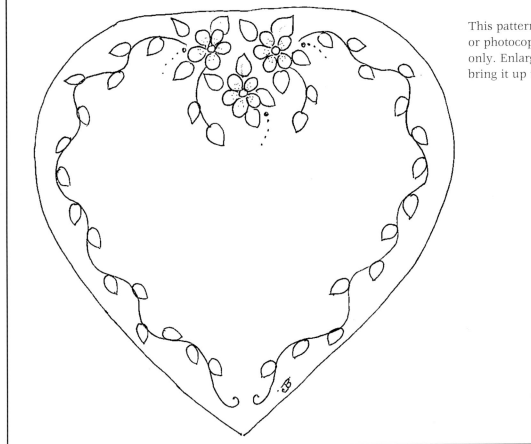

This pattern may be hand-traced or photocopied for personal use only. Enlarge at 147 percent to bring it up to full size.

Add the Flowers

5 Add the large dot in the center of the flowers with Pale Yellow on the tip end of your brush handle. With the smallest end of your stylus, dip into the still wet yellow center dot.

6 Walk tiny stamen dots around the main dot and out onto the petals.

7 Finally, add a spray of Pale Yellow diminishing dots coming out from each flower in a gently curving line. Allow to dry completely. Remove the transfer lines with a damp paper towel. Spray on a satin varnish.

Completed Lid

Lilac Folk Art Box

Project Five

Ice Storm Violet   Pale Lilac   Lilac   Deep Lilac   Eggplant

PAINT Delta Ceramcoat Acrylics. **SURFACE** Small wooden keepsake box, available at any craft store. **BRUSHES** no. 4 filbert • 18/0 liner. **ADDITIONAL SUPPLIES** Wood sealer • Sanding pad • Tack cloth • Tracing paper • Stylus • Blue Super Chacopaper • Satin varnish.

1 Remove the brass clasp and hinges that come on the box to keep them clean. Prepare the wooden box for painting by first sealing it, then sanding it with a little round sanding pad. Wipe off the sanding dust with a tack cloth.

Basecoat the entire box with Ice Storm Violet. Base the two side panels with Pale Lilac.

Transfer the Pattern and Paint the Lid

This pattern may be hand-traced or photocopied for personal use only. Enlarge at 143 percent to bring up to full size.

2 Transfer the pattern onto the top of the lid using a stylus and blue Super Chacopaper. Start the center design by painting the back petals of the tulips with Eggplant. Paint the two side tulips with Lilac, and the center tulip with Deep Lilac. The little strokes at the base of the tulips are painted in Eggplant with the liner brush.

3 Paint the tulip stems, the scrolls and the two hooks at the top of the two side tulips with Eggplant.

4 With Deep Lilac on a liner, paint 2 hook strokes coming off the base of each of the side tulip stems. With Lilac, paint 4 hook strokes coming off the stem of the center tulip.

5 Make a large dot with Eggplant at the center bottom, and a smaller Pale Lilac dot at the base of each tulip. This completes the center design. Around the perimeter of the lid, freehand a mini scalloped border with Lilac on a no. 4 filbert.

Complete the Lid, Box Front and Sides

6 Paint a thin line on the inside edge of the scallop border with Deep Lilac on a liner brush. This helps hide any ragged edges. In each corner, paint two overlapping C-strokes with a liner and Deep Lilac. Finish off with a large dot of Eggplant.

The design on the lid is a mirror image, so turn the lid around and complete the other half of the design by following steps 2 through 5. After all sides of the box are completed, allow the paint to dry. Remove the transfer lines with a damp paper towel. Use a satin spray varnish to protect the box. Replace the brass hinges and clasp.

Completed Box Side

Completed Lid

Completed Box Front

Pink Tulip Tray

Project 6

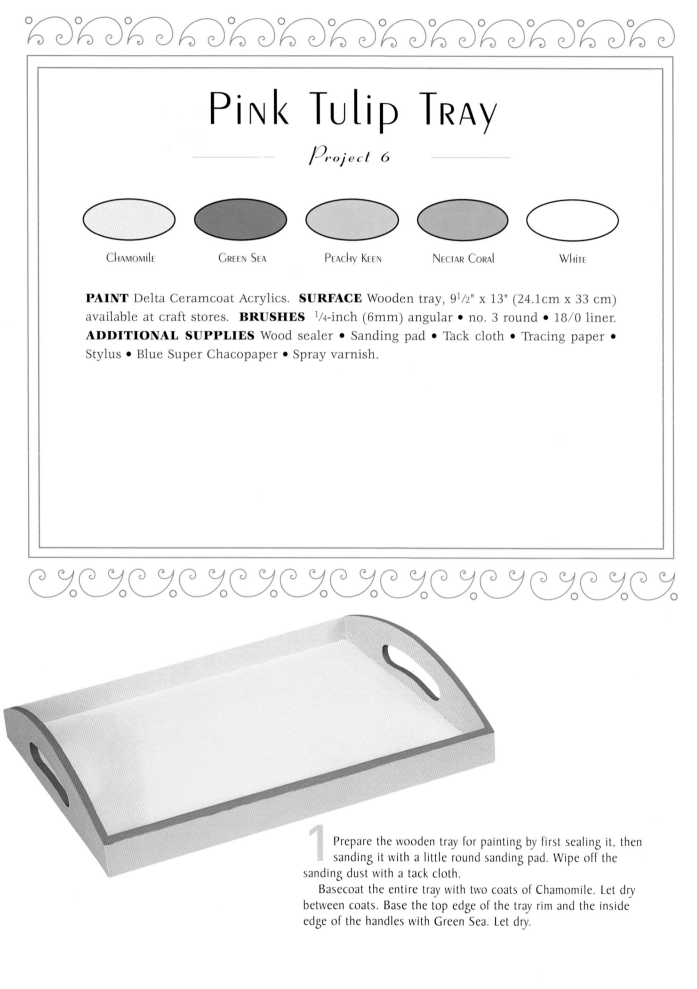

| Chamomile | Green Sea | Peachy Keen | Nectar Coral | White |

PAINT Delta Ceramcoat Acrylics. **SURFACE** Wooden tray, 9½" x 13" (24.1cm x 33 cm) available at craft stores. **BRUSHES** ¼-inch (6mm) angular • no. 3 round • 18/0 liner. **ADDITIONAL SUPPLIES** Wood sealer • Sanding pad • Tack cloth • Tracing paper • Stylus • Blue Super Chacopaper • Spray varnish.

1 Prepare the wooden tray for painting by first sealing it, then sanding it with a little round sanding pad. Wipe off the sanding dust with a tack cloth.

Basecoat the entire tray with two coats of Chamomile. Let dry between coats. Base the top edge of the tray rim and the inside edge of the handles with Green Sea. Let dry.

Making a Pattern for a Repeating Design

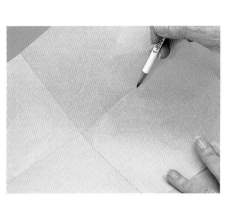

2 Measure a piece of tracing paper to lay flat inside the tray. Trim it to fit.

3 Remove the tracing paper from the tray and fold it into quarters. Unfold it and draw a light pencil line along the fold lines.

4 Measure 2 inches (51mm) in from the outside edge of the paper in $^1/_2$-inch (12mm) increments on all four sides. Make dots at each increment, then draw pencil lines to connect the dots. These are your guidelines.

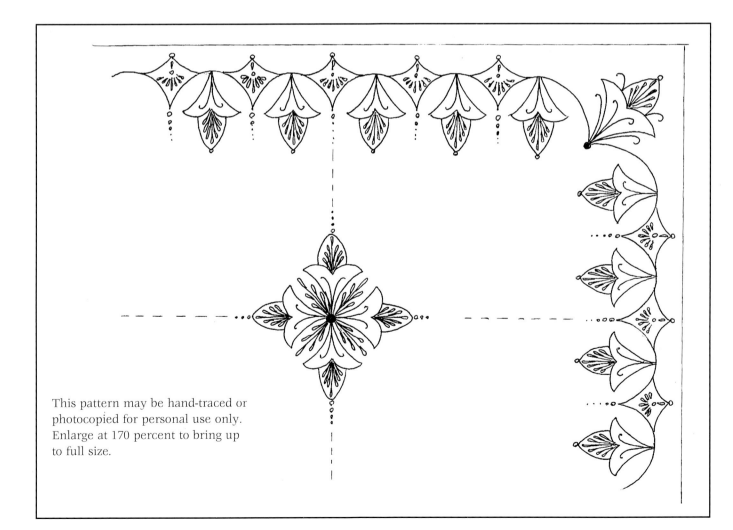

This pattern may be hand-traced or photocopied for personal use only. Enlarge at 170 percent to bring up to full size.

5 Fold one corner of the tracing paper in on itself to create a 45° angle from corner to corner of the guidelines.

6 Open up the tracing paper and draw one-half of the corner tulip motif on one-half of the corner you just folded.

7 Refold the corner, and on the other half of the paper, trace the design you just drew in step 6. This completes your corner design.

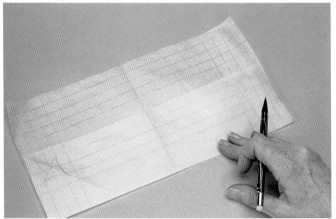

8 To evenly space the tulip motifs along the short side of the pattern, crease the tracing paper, aligning the innermost line on the long side with the center crease of the whole sheet lengthwise. Repeat these creases every one inch (25mm).

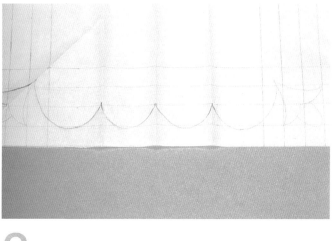

9 Trace the tulip motif in the other corner. Draw curved lines from crease to crease, joining them to the base of the tulip motif in each corner.

10 Draw a V-shaped line from base to base of the curved lines. Draw a tulip motif in between each of the folds on one quarter of the tracing paper. Fold the paper over on the center fold and trace the other quarter of the design. This completes the spine of your border design.

11 Add the details and embellishments to the pattern as shown here: commas, dots and hooks. It might be helpful to compare your pattern to the finished painting on page 49 to see how these details look in the design.

12 Transfer the pattern onto the tray bottom using a stylus and blue Super Chacopaper.

Begin Painting the Tulips

13 Using a ¼-inch (6mm) angular brush, basecoat the back petal of each tulip with Peachy Keen and the front petals with Nectar Coral.

14 With Sea Green on a liner brush, paint the large curving lines that contain each tulip, following the pattern you traced on. If you used the Super Chacopaper to transfer your pattern, you can paint right over the traced lines.

Add Embellishments

15 Load a liner brush with White and outline the upper back sections of the tulips. Add White hook strokes to the tulip fronts and seven comma strokes to the tulip backs—a long center stroke and 3 shorter strokes on each side. In the spaces between the tulips, paint 7 tiny White daisy petals in an arch shape.

16 Load a liner with Green Sea and add hook strokes to either side of the corner tulip. Below each daisy, add a leaf and a dot. Dot in the daisy centers with Peachy Keen. Dot the tops of the tulip backs and the top and base of each corner tulip with Nectar Coral. Finally, add 5 diminishing dots of White coming out from the points of the green lines. Repeat this process on the other three corners of the tray.

Paint the Center Medallion

17 The center medallion is simply a repeat of the tulip motif used around the border—4 tulips whose bases meet in the center. The colors are the same. Divide the 4 tulips with long strokes of Green Sea and a center dot. Add 2 shorter White strokes on each side, and 4 diminishing dots from the back petal point. Allow to dry completely. Remove transfer lines with a damp paper towel. Use spray varnish to protect the tray.

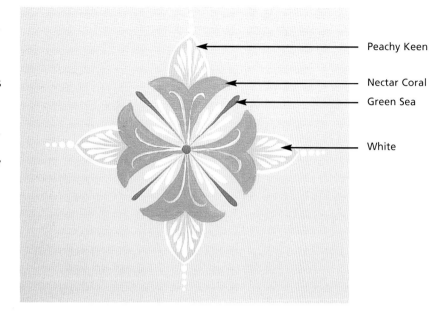

Peachy Keen

Nectar Coral

Green Sea

White

Completed Tray

Two-toned Round Plate

Project Seven

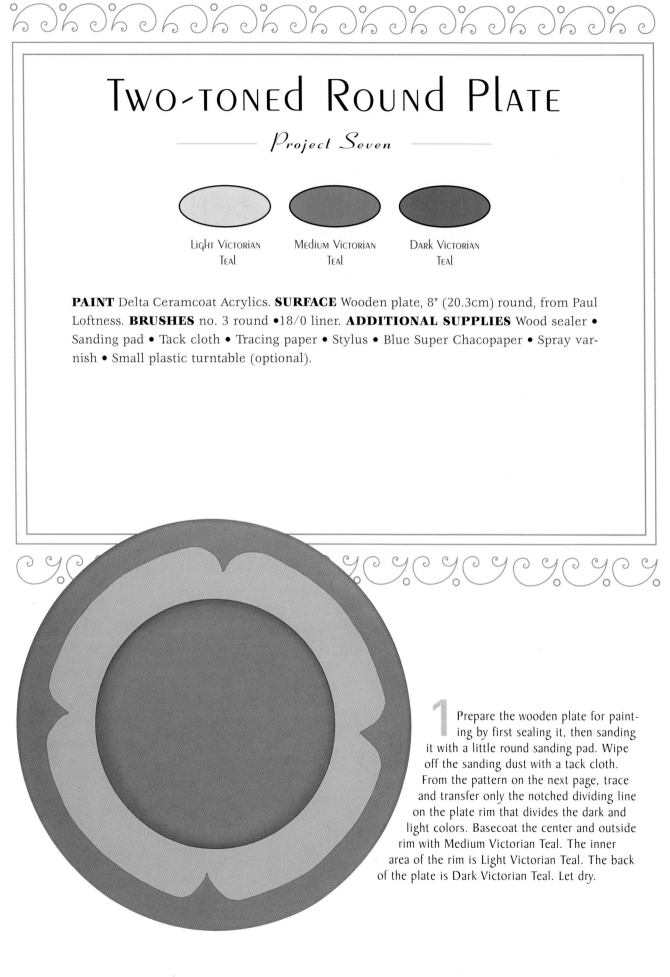

Light Victorian Teal

Medium Victorian Teal

Dark Victorian Teal

PAINT Delta Ceramcoat Acrylics. **SURFACE** Wooden plate, 8" (20.3cm) round, from Paul Loftness. **BRUSHES** no. 3 round •18/0 liner. **ADDITIONAL SUPPLIES** Wood sealer • Sanding pad • Tack cloth • Tracing paper • Stylus • Blue Super Chacopaper • Spray varnish • Small plastic turntable (optional).

1 Prepare the wooden plate for painting by first sealing it, then sanding it with a little round sanding pad. Wipe off the sanding dust with a tack cloth. From the pattern on the next page, trace and transfer only the notched dividing line on the plate rim that divides the dark and light colors. Basecoat the center and outside rim with Medium Victorian Teal. The inner area of the rim is Light Victorian Teal. The back of the plate is Dark Victorian Teal. Let dry.

Paint the Repeating Border Design

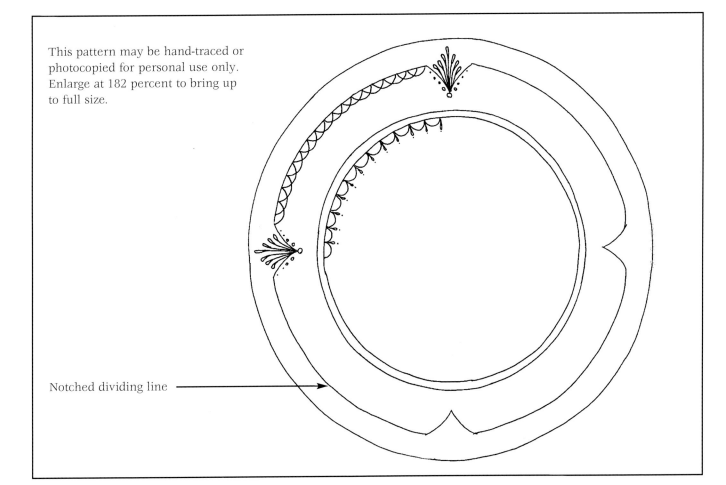

This pattern may be hand-traced or photocopied for personal use only. Enlarge at 182 percent to bring up to full size.

Notched dividing line

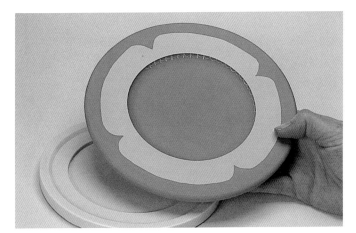

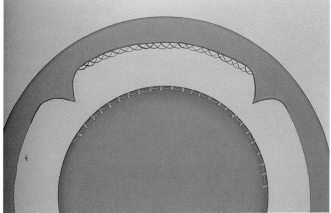

2 Trace and transfer the rest of the pattern to the basecoated plate. For many border designs, it's easier to paint repeating patterns if you set your surface on a small plastic turntable or lazy susan. Begin on the inside rim of the center area with little scallops separated by tiny commas painted in Light Victorian Teal on a liner brush.

3 With Dark Victorian Teal on a liner brush, paint little crossover scallops along the division between the darker and lighter areas on the rim. Then add a thin band of the same color along that dividing line.

Add Embellishments

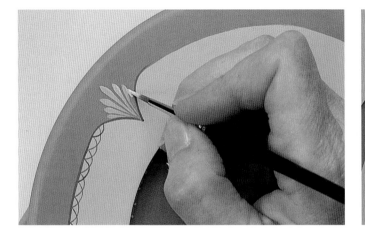

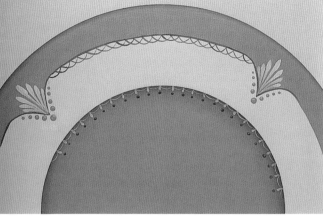

4 Load a liner brush with Light Victorian Teal. In each V-shaped notch, paint a fan shape of 7 comma or teardrop-shaped strokes. The longest one is in the middle, with 3 shorter ones on either side.

5 On the inner rim, add tiny dots of Dark Victorian teal at the base of each tiny comma stroke. Since these dots are so little, it may be easier to use the small end of a stylus. On the rim under the fan strokes, add a large dot at the base with Medium Victorian Teal, and 3 dots of diminishing size up each side. When the paint is completely dry, remove your transfer lines and varnish the plate to protect it.

Completed Plate

COUNTRY KITCHEN RECIPE BOX

Project Eight

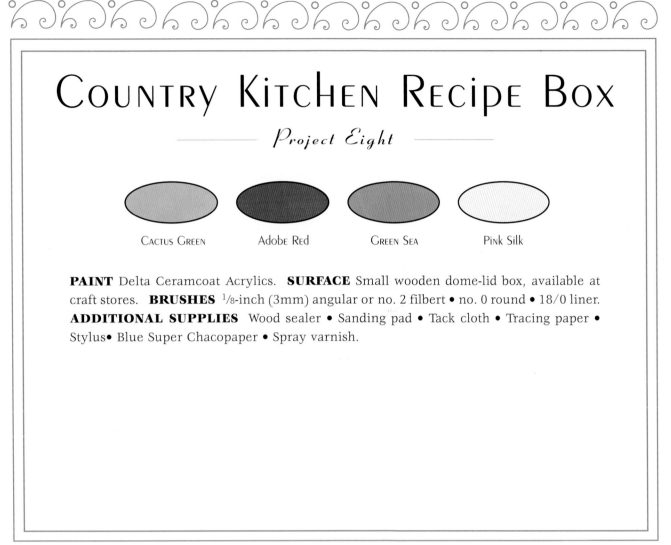

CACTUS GREEN	Adobe Red	GREEN SEA	Pink Silk

PAINT Delta Ceramcoat Acrylics. **SURFACE** Small wooden dome-lid box, available at craft stores. **BRUSHES** ⅛-inch (3mm) angular or no. 2 filbert • no. 0 round • 18/0 liner. **ADDITIONAL SUPPLIES** Wood sealer • Sanding pad • Tack cloth • Tracing paper • Stylus• Blue Super Chacopaper • Spray varnish.

1 Remove the brass hinges and clasp to keep them clean. Prepare the wooden box for painting by first sealing it, then sanding it with a little round sanding pad. Wipe off the sanding dust with a tack cloth.

Basecoat the entire box with Cactus Green. Sand lightly and apply a second coat. Base the side bands with Adobe Red.

Transfer the Pattern and Paint the Lid

2 Begin the center medallion by transferring the pattern to the center of the domed lid. Paint four 3-lobed leaves with Green Sea on a round brush. Let dry. Paint the five-petal center flower with Adobe Red. Between each leaf, add a fan shape of three comma strokes with Pink Silk on a liner brush.

3 Finish the center medallion with a circle of diminishing Pink Silk dots in the center of the red flower. Use the small end of a stylus to make dots this tiny. With the tip end of a brush handle, add a large dot of Adobe Red at the base of each of the fan-shaped commas. In the four corners of the center area of the lid, paint 3 commas in a fan shape with Pink Silk and add a dot at the base with Green Sea (see the Completed Lid on the facing page).

Begin the side bands by transferring the pattern for the flower shapes. Paint the 3-lobed leaves in each 4-leaf set with Green Sea. Let dry.

This pattern may be hand-traced or photocopied for personal use only. Enlarge at 118 percent to bring up to full size.

Complete the Lid and Front of Box

4 With Pink Silk on a no. 0 round, paint 4 sets of three fan-shaped comma strokes between the green leaves you just painted. Let dry. In the centers, paint a 5-dot flower and a dot separating each flower section with Adobe Red on the large end of a stylus. For uniformity of size, dip the stylus into paint for each dot. Let dry.

5 In the center of each 5-dot flower, add a dot of Pink Silk. Extend the border design down the front and back of the box to finish it off, being careful to align the design where the lid opens. Allow to dry completely. Remove any transfer lines and protect the box with varnish. Replace the brass clasp and hinges.

Completed Lid

Completed Box Front

Rose Oval Board

Project Nine

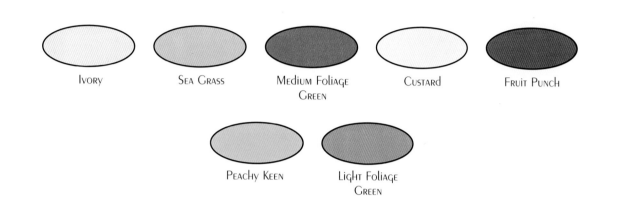

IVORY   SEA GRASS   MEDIUM FOLIAGE GREEN   CUSTARD   FRUIT PUNCH

PEACHY KEEN   LIGHT FOLIAGE GREEN

PAINT Delta Ceramcoat Acrylics. **SURFACE** Oval wooden board with routered inset, 15" x 21" (38.1cm x 53.3 cm), from Stan Brown Arts & Crafts catalog. **BRUSHES** ⅛-inch (6mm) angular • no. 3 round • 18/0 liner • no. 2 filbert. **ADDITIONAL SUPPLIES** Wood sealer • Sanding pad • Tack cloth • Tracing paper • Stylus • Blue Super Chacopaper • Gray chalk pencil • Spray varnish.

1 Prepare the wooden board for painting by first sealing it, then sanding it with a sanding pad. Wipe off the sanding dust with a tack cloth.

Basecoat the entire board with two coats of Ivory. Let dry between coats. Base the routered inset with Medium Foliage Green. Base the outside rim with Sea Grass. Base the inside band with Custard. This inside band is 1½ inches (38mm) wide, measured from the edge of the routered inset.

Patterns for Rim Border, Rosebud Border and Rose Center

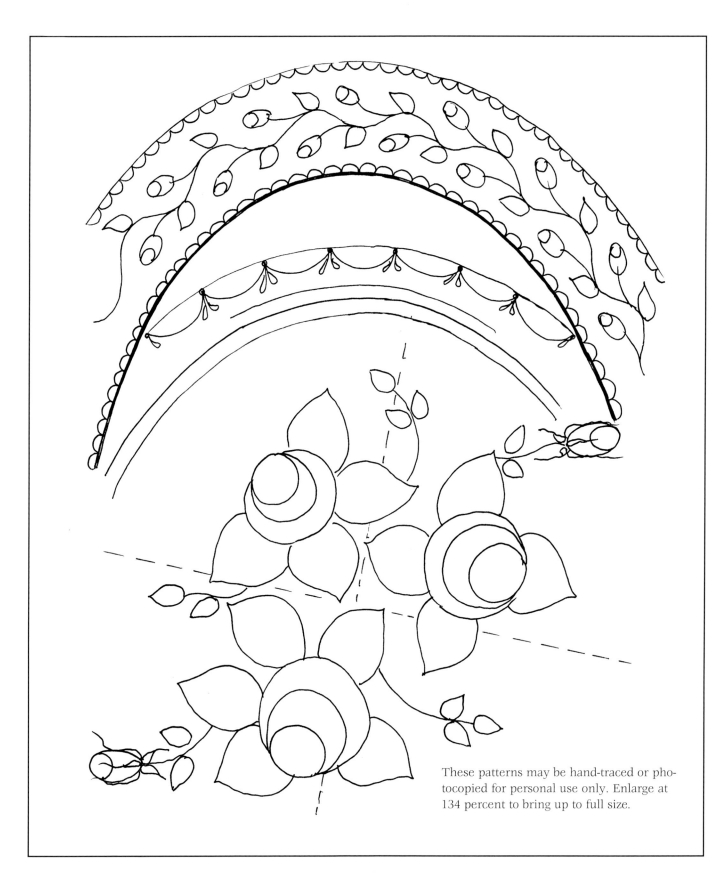

These patterns may be hand-traced or photocopied for personal use only. Enlarge at 134 percent to bring up to full size.

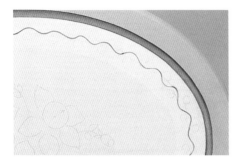

2 Transfer the rosebud border pattern to the Custard band. Paint the rosebud border lifeline around the entire band with Medium Foliage Green on an 18/0 liner brush.

3 On your palette, double load a ¼-inch (6mm) angular brush with Fruit Punch on the heel (short side) of the brush and Peachy Keen on the toe (long side) of the brush.

4 Blend on your palette.

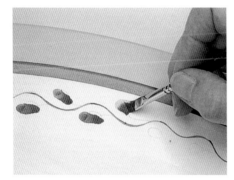

5 To paint each rosebud, start with the back petal and paint a small C-stroke, keeping the lighter color toward the top.

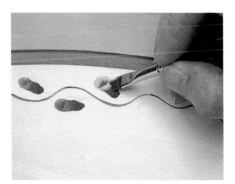

6 Paint the front petal with a little V-shaped stroke. Don't worry if the base of the bud is a little ragged—the calyx will cover it up.

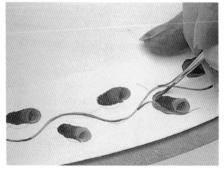

7 To paint the calyxes, turn the board so you're pulling your brush toward you. Load a liner with Medium Foliage Green and pull a stroke up each side of the bud. The stroke should be fatter at the base and taper off as it comes around the top of the bud.

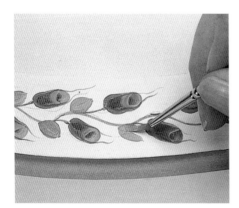

8 Paint small two-stroke leaves along the vine with a liner brush mix of Medium Foliage Green and Light Foliage Green.

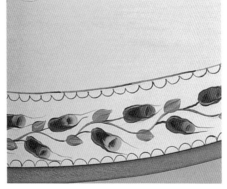

9 Load a liner with Fruit Punch and freehand lacy scallops along each side of the Custard band. Add a fine line of Medium Foliage Green.

Paint Border on Outside Rim

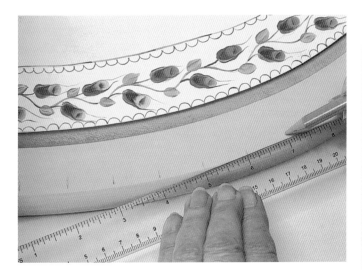

10 For the outermost border on the very edge of the green rim, mark off 1-inch (25mm) intervals with a ruler and gray chalk pencil all around the board.

11 Paint arching scallops between the 1-inch (25mm) marks with Medium Foliage Green on an 18/0 liner. Strive to keep the depth of the scallops uniform around the entire rim.

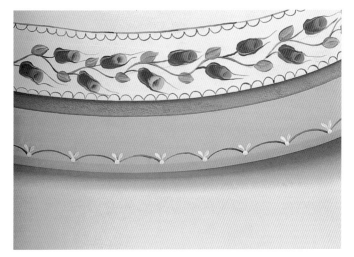

12 Add two small comma strokes in the V of the scallops with Custard on an 18/0 liner. At the base of each, add a dot of Ivory with the stylus. Let dry completely.

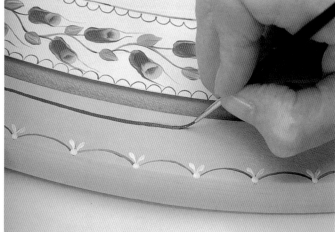

13 With a gray chalk pencil, draw a line about ¼ inch (6mm) away from the darker green routered inset all around the rim. Following this chalk line, paint the line with Fruit Punch on an 18/0 liner, laid flat to make a thicker line. Let dry.

Completed Borders and Center Rose Leaves

14 Here is the completed board showing the inside border of rosebuds and the outside border along the edge. You may stop with just the borders if you wish, or continue on with the center design of coral roses and green leaves, which are shown step-by-step in the photos below and on the next two pages. After all of the painting is complete, let it dry thoroughly. Use a spray varnish to protect the board. The design on this board is such that it looks fine displayed either horizontally as shown here, or vertically as shown on page 58.

15 Transfer the pattern for the roses and leaves to the center of the board. Double load an angular brush with Light Foliage Green on the toe (long side) and Medium Foliage Green on the heel (short side). Blend on the palette. Paint one half of the leaf, sliding the brush back and forth to create the look of veining. Keep the light green to the outside.

16 Repeat for the other half of the leaf. Let dry. Sideload the toe of the angular brush into Dark Foliage Green and paint a wash down the center of each leaf, curving it slightly. This is the shading for the center vein.

17 Sideload the toe of the angular brush into Light Foliage Green and paint a highlight down the center of each leaf. With Dark Foliage Green, reinforce the center vein and add the stems.

CENTER ROSE STEP by STEP

USING A CLOCK FACE TO PAINT A ROSE

This method of painting a rose makes it easy to know where to put each petal. Just follow each step as shown on these two pages. Notice that these petals are not made with smooth brushstrokes. Allow them to be a little imperfect looking.

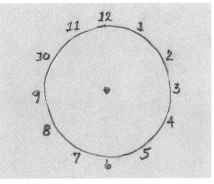

1 Draw a clock face with a dot in the middle.

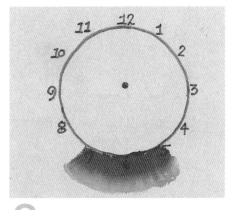

2 Double load an angular brush with Fruit Punch and Peachy Keen (see page 61) and stroke in the first petal from 5 to 7. Keep the light color to the outside.

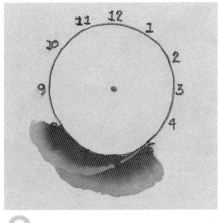

3 Reload and stroke in the second petal starting at 8 and tapering off at 5.

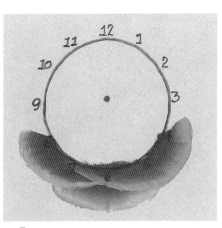

4 Repeat the same stroke starting at 4 and tapering off at 7.

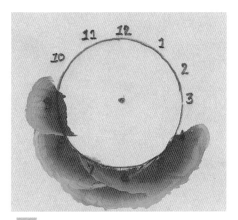

5 Reload and pull a short stroke from 9 to 8.

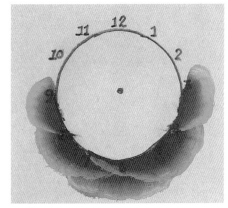

6 Repeat the stroke from 3 to 4.

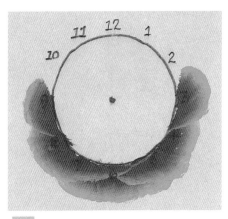

7 Notice the angle of the above stroke between the circle and the stroke—it forms a small V shape.

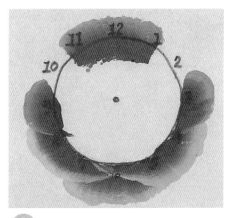

8 Reload and paint a curved stroke straddling the circle from 11 to 1.

COMPLETE THE CENTER ROSE

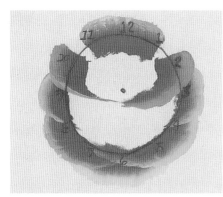

9 Reload and set your brush down just above 2. Press and pull across the circle to beneath the center dot, catching the outside corner of the 3 to 4 stroke. Repeat on the other side from 10 to 9.

10 Reload and paint short strokes in the upper back from 1 to 2 and 10 to 11. Work your way toward the front, painting short filler strokes in the center and longer C-strokes at the sides with tails that end at the center dot.

11 Paint the innermost petal of the front of the bowl, connecting the tail at the dot with a slide-press-slide.

12 Add more petals to the front of the bowl. Each stroke goes from side to side.

13 Complete the front petals of the bowl by filling in over any background that is still showing.

14 Overpaint smaller filler petals to complete the front of the rose. Don't crisscross the strokes; pull them from side to side.

Add stamens to the inside bowl and finish with leaves.

Wall Border & Picture Frame

Project Ten

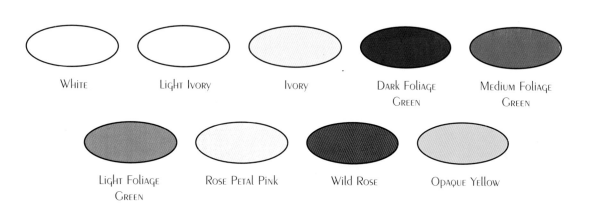

White	Light Ivory	Ivory	Dark Foliage Green	Medium Foliage Green

Light Foliage Green	Rose Petal Pink	Wild Rose	Opaque Yellow

PAINT Delta Ceramcoat Acrylics. **SURFACE** Painted interior wall with window • Large oval wooden picture frame with center insert, 18" x 26 ¹/₂" (45.7cm x 67.3cm), from Stan Brown Arts & Crafts catalog. **BRUSHES** ³/₈-inch (9mm) angular • no. 0 round • 10/0 liner • 18/0 liner • nos. 2 and 6 filberts. **ADDITIONAL SUPPLIES** ´Wood sealer • Sanding pad • Tack cloth • Tracing paper • Stylus • Blue Super Chacopaper • Yardstick (meterstick) or ruler • Level • Chalk pencils • Spray varnish (for picture frame).

1 The pretty and feminine daisy border that frames the window in the room at left can also be painted on a smaller scale on this oval picture frame. They make a nice ensemble that pulls the room together. On the center insert board, I painted a series of repeating border patterns to set off a botanical print I found at a home goods store. Instructions for painting the oval frame begin on page 75.

Measuring the Wall for the Daisy Border

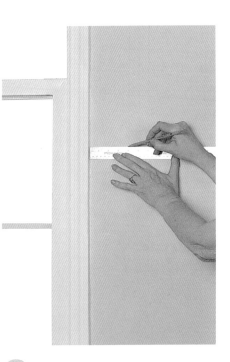

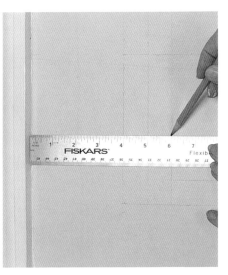

1 Before beginning the daisy wall border, prepare the wall area around the window by washing it with a cleaner suitable for flat wall paint. If you want to change the wall color, use an interior grade latex with a flat or eggshell finish. Remove any curtains from the window.

2 First decide how long and wide you want your daisy border to be. Then measure out from the outside of the window frame to determine the centerline of your design. Allow room for any curtains, tiebacks or other window treatments you will be using when the project is finished.

3 The width of this border design is 2 inches (5.1 cm) and the centerline is 5 inches (12.7 cm) out from the window frame. Measure and mark the wall at the 4-inch (10.2 cm), 5-inch (12.7 cm) and 6-inch (15.2 cm) distances from the window frame with a chalk pencil. (Here I'm using a regular lead pencil so you can see the lines more easily). Use a level or ruler to draw these lines all around the window frame. These are the left and right boundary lines and the centerline of your daisy border design.

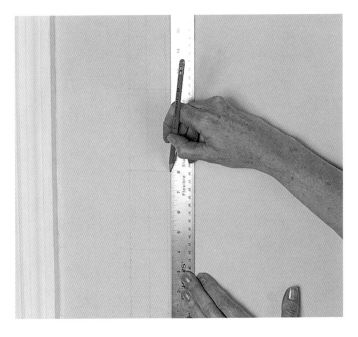

4 Each daisy-and-stem section is 4 inches (10.2 cm) long, so divide your 2-inch (5.1 cm) wide band into 4-inch (10.2 cm) sections all the way around the window frame and draw chalk lines across the band.

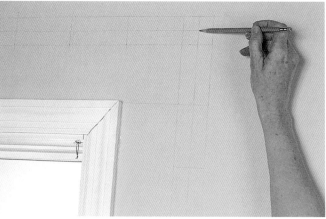

5 In this project, the vertical daisy design along the window frame joins a horizontal wall border about two-thirds of the way down the window frame (see the photo on page 66). Above you can see the inner pivot point where the vertical band joins the horizontal band.

6 Here is the outer pivot point where the vertical band makes a 90° turn to the left over the top of the window.

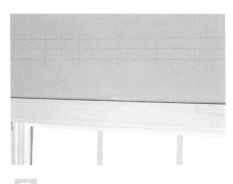

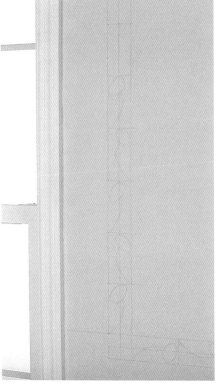

7 When I divided the top band into 4-inch (10.2 cm) sections, I ended up with an even number (10) of sections. I made a little "V" to mark the halfway point.

8 Lightly pencil in the outlines of each daisy section within the boundary lines you've already marked on the wall. Freehand an elliptical shape for each daisy blossom, and a long curving line for each stem.

9 For this design, the daisies face in alternate directions, so the curving stems form a wavy line. This wavy line is the spine of the design.

Paint the Daisy Blossoms

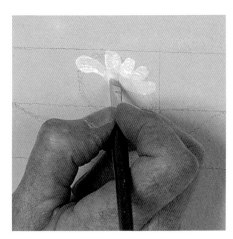

10 To paint the border, begin with the daisy petals. Load a no. 6 filbert brush with White and paint the back petals. Then paint a curving transition petal on one side.

11 Paint a curving transition petal on the other side.

12 Continue around to paint the front petals, curving them in toward the blossom center.

13 Paint the final front petal.

14 Here you can see how the daisy blossoms alternate direction as they go along the vertical side of the window frame and along the wall border. Every so often, paint an overlapping petal to give a more natural look, and so your daisies look handpainted rather than stamped or stencilled on the wall.

Add the Daisy Centers and the Stems

15 With Opaque Yellow on a no. 6 filbert brush, paint the daisy centers in the shape of a rounded oval, overlapping the bases of the back petals slightly. If two coats are needed for coverage, let the first coat dry before applying the second.

16 Load Dark Foliage Green on a 10/0 liner brush. Paint each curving stem by starting at the daisy petals and pulling a tapered line toward the end of the stem.

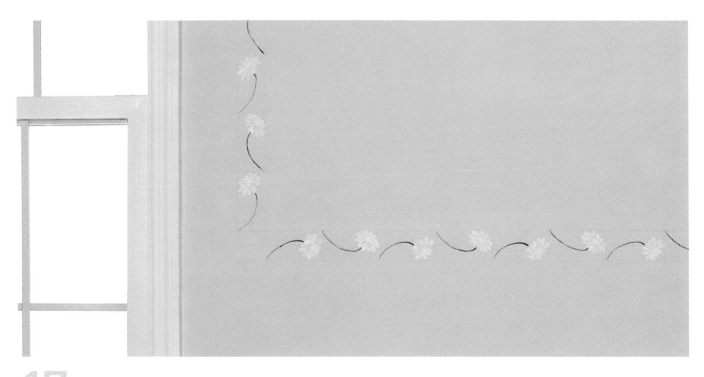

17 Alternate the curve of each stem as you go along, and note the direction of the curves in the corner where the design takes a 90° turn up the wall.

Add Embellishments

18 To shade and separate the yellow daisy centers from the front petals, load a 10/0 liner brush with Dark Foliage Green and paint a thin C-stroke as shown. This helps give the yellow centers a rounded look.

19 On your palette, make a brush mix of Medium and Light Foliage Green. With a 10/0 liner, freehand a scroll line and a hook stroke coming off the base of the stem.

20 Keep the scroll line and hook stroke on the same side of the curve of the stem. If the daisy head is facing up, paint the strokes on the upper side of the stem. If the daisy is facing down, paint the strokes on the underside of the stem.

Paint the Tendrils and the Corner Leaves

21 If you wish to add a little more color and an extra flourish to your border, paint a thin curling tendril around the daisy stems with Wild Rose on a 10/0 liner.

22 At the inside pivot point where the vertical border meets the horizontal border, paint a simple 3-leaf design with a brush mix of Dark, Medium and Light Foliage Green on a no. 6 filbert.

23 Texture the leaves with Light Foliage Green vein lines. To tie the corner leaf design to the two borders, add a couple of tendrils with the same green mixture on a 10/0 liner.

24 At the outer pivot point where the vertical border makes a 90° turn over the top of the window frame, paint another 3-leaf design with the same green mix as in steps 22 and 23. Add two tendrils to connect to the borders.

25 In the center of the border over the top of the window frame, paint a two-leaf design and add a couple of tendrils curving over toward the center in a sort of heart shape.

COMPLETED WALL BORDER

26 The leaf and tendril designs in the corners and at the center top help draw attention to the 90° turns in the border and give it a neat and finished appearance. When your design is finished and all the paint is completely dry, use an art gum eraser to remove your chalk pencil lines. If needed, touch up boo-boos with your wall color paint.

Daisy Border Picture Frame

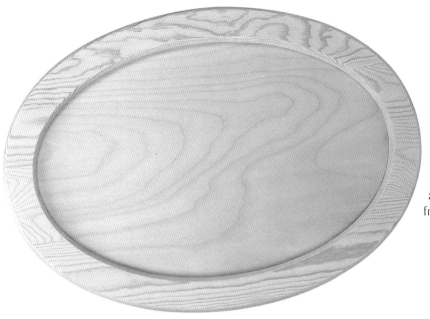

1 Seal the oval wooden frame and the center insert with wood sealer. Sand them with a sanding pad, then wipe off the sanding dust with a tack cloth. The center insert can be detached from the outer frame for easier sanding.

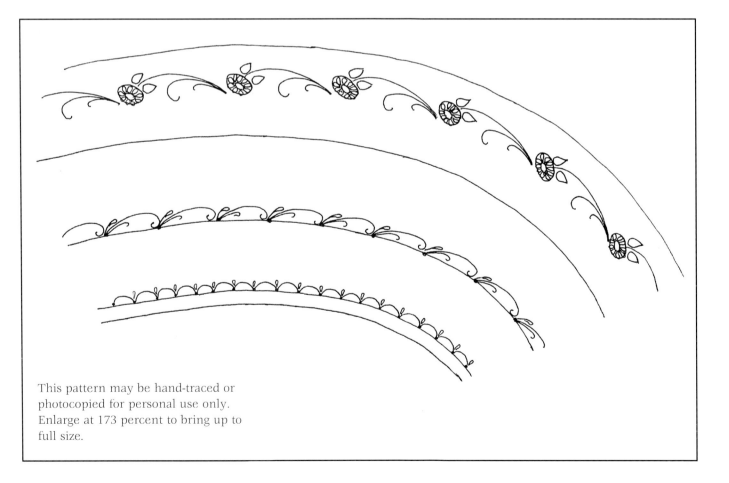

This pattern may be hand-traced or photocopied for personal use only. Enlarge at 173 percent to bring up to full size.

Paint the Daisies on the Outer Frame

2 Basecoat the frame with two coats of Wild Rose, sanding lightly between coats. Let dry. Transfer the daisy pattern on the previous page to the frame.

Paint the daisy petals using a no. 0 round and White. Double load a ⅜-inch (9mm) angular brush with Light Foliage Green and Medium Foliage Green and paint the two little leaves, making some of them darker and some lighter. Let dry.

The daisy centers are Opaque Yellow with a dot of White for a highlight. Paint a small shadow line at the base of each center with thinned Medium Foliage Green on an 18/0 liner.

The stems are Dark Foliage Green and the hook strokes coming off the stems are a brush mix of Dark and Medium Foliage Green.

The artwork in the center is a print I found at a home goods store. I just cut it into an oval and glued it to the center insert. An old-fashioned photograph or a drawing would look just as nice.

Paint the Middle and Inner Borders

3 Before beginning the borders on the wooden insert inside the frame, basecoat the entire center insert with two coats of Light Ivory. Sand lightly between coats. Let dry.

Basecoat the outer 1 1/2-inch (38mm) wide band in Rose Petal Pink. Let dry. (Part of this band is hidden behind the inner rim of the daisy frame in the photo at right).

Basecoat the inner 1-inch (25mm) band in Ivory. Let dry.

Mark off 1-inch (25mm) increments around the inside of the entire Rose Petal Pink band. Paint dots on each mark with Medium Foliage Green, then paint connecting scrolls with the same color on an 18/0 liner. The two little hook strokes are Wild Rose.

The innermost border on the Ivory band is just a series of scallop lines, dots and teardrop-shaped strokes. Measure and mark every 1/2 inch (12mm) around the inside of the Ivory band. Paint scallops from mark to mark with Medium Foliage Green on an 18/0 liner. Add small teardrop strokes of Dark Foliage Green all around. Finish off with a dot of Wild Rose between each scallop.

Allow the paint to dry completely. Remove any visible transfer and chalk lines, then varnish to protect your painting. Once the varnish is dry, then add a coordinating print or photo to the very center.

33 Borders in 3 Easy Steps

KITCHEN

1 Base in the bowl of the teacups and teapot with medium blue.

2 Shade the teapot and cups with a darker blue. Paint the teapot's knob, handle and base, and the saucers with dark blue.

3 Highlight the cups and pot and add the flowers with white.

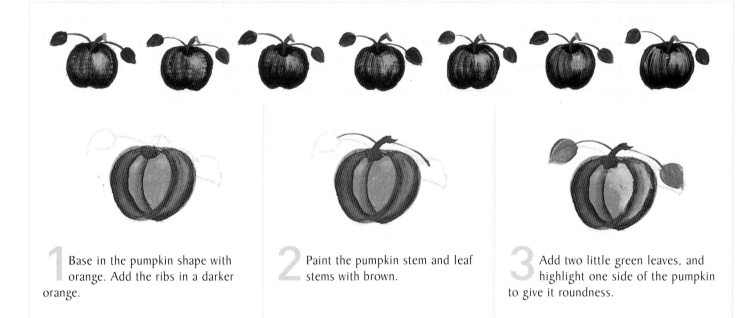

1 Base in the pumpkin shape with orange. Add the ribs in a darker orange.

2 Paint the pumpkin stem and leaf stems with brown.

3 Add two little green leaves, and highlight one side of the pumpkin to give it roundness.

KitcHen

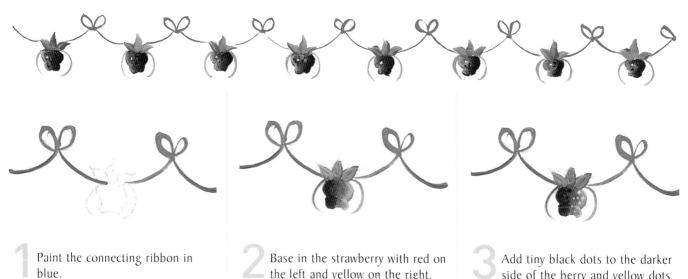

1 Paint the connecting ribbon in blue.

2 Base in the strawberry with red on the left and yellow on the right. Blend in the middle. Add two little green tendrils and three hull leaves.

3 Add tiny black dots to the darker side of the berry and yellow dots on the lighter side.

1 Base in the bowl in medium blue and the spoons in light brown. Add a white oval for the inside of the bowl.

2 Shade the bowls and handles of the spoons with medium brown. Shade the outside of the bowl with dark blue, and the inside with lighter blue.

3 Paint the checkerboard squares with bright red and white. Add white trim to the bowl if desired.

Ribbons and Tassels

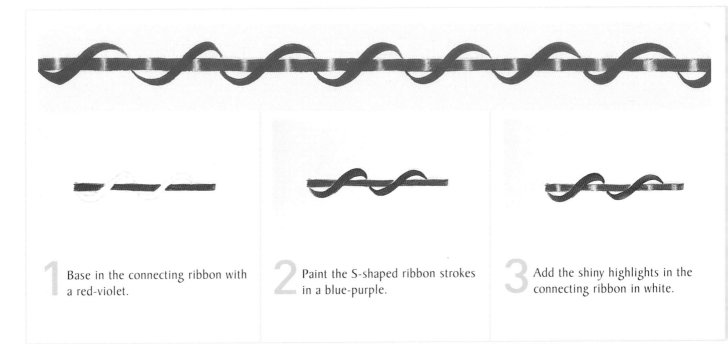

1 Base in the connecting ribbon with a red-violet.

2 Paint the S-shaped ribbon strokes in a blue-purple.

3 Add the shiny highlights in the connecting ribbon in white.

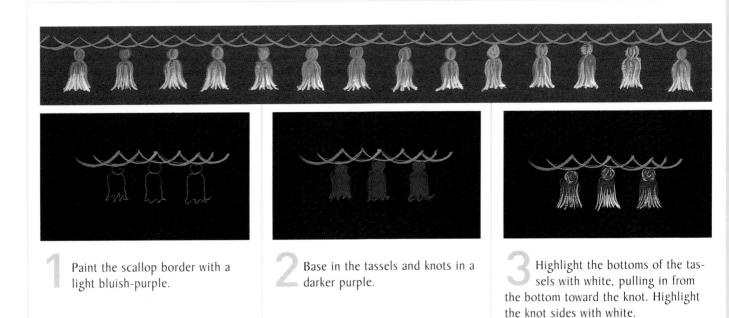

1 Paint the scallop border with a light bluish-purple.

2 Base in the tassels and knots in a darker purple.

3 Highlight the bottoms of the tassels with white, pulling in from the bottom toward the knot. Highlight the knot sides with white.

COUNTRY

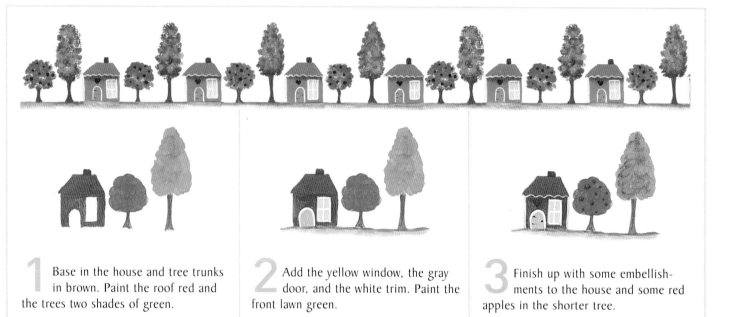

1 Base in the house and tree trunks in brown. Paint the roof red and the trees two shades of green.

2 Add the yellow window, the gray door, and the white trim. Paint the front lawn green.

3 Finish up with some embellishments to the house and some red apples in the shorter tree.

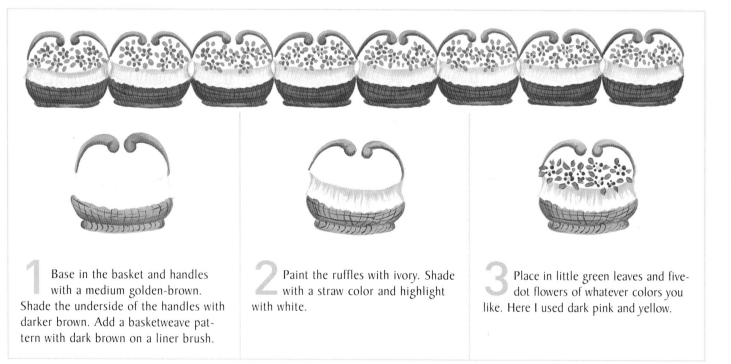

1 Base in the basket and handles with a medium golden-brown. Shade the underside of the handles with darker brown. Add a basketweave pattern with dark brown on a liner brush.

2 Paint the ruffles with ivory. Shade with a straw color and highlight with white.

3 Place in little green leaves and five-dot flowers of whatever colors you like. Here I used dark pink and yellow.

Floral Garlands

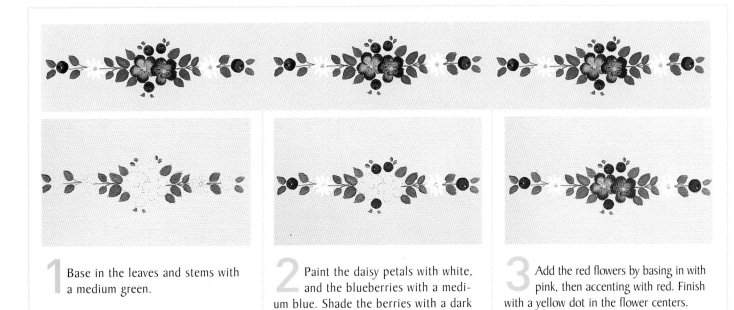

1 Base in the leaves and stems with a medium green.

2 Paint the daisy petals with white, and the blueberries with a medium blue. Shade the berries with a dark blue and add a white highlight dot.

3 Add the red flowers by basing in with pink, then accenting with red. Finish with a yellow dot in the flower centers.

1 Paint the connecting linework in light green and light pink, using a small liner brush.

2 Paint the four-petal flowers in pink, and the curved strokes and commas in green.

3 Finish with red dots and green diminishing dots.

Floral Garlands

1 Base in the inner rose petal with medium pink. Paint the leaves with a brush mix of medium and dark green.

2 With a darker pink, shade in the throat of the rose and the "V"shape between the two side petals, which are a mix of pink and white. Dot in the buds with dark red.

3 Add the connecting lines and stems with green.

1 Stipple in the heart shapes with dark green, then again in light green. Paint the two lower leaves with a brush mix of dark and light green.

2 With a deep coral pink, paint the top and bottom bands of the design, the C-strokes and the random pink dots on the green hearts.

3 Finish with diminishing white dots in both directions between the pink C-strokes, and random white dots on the green hearts. Paint a white curving line to connect the hearts and daisies.

Kids

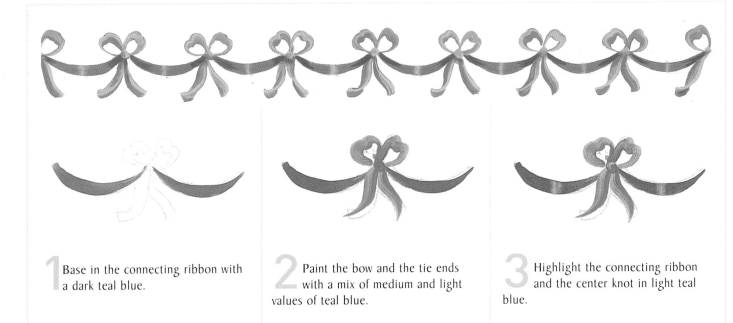

1 Base in the connecting ribbon with a dark teal blue.

2 Paint the bow and the tie ends with a mix of medium and light values of teal blue.

3 Highlight the connecting ribbon and the center knot in light teal blue.

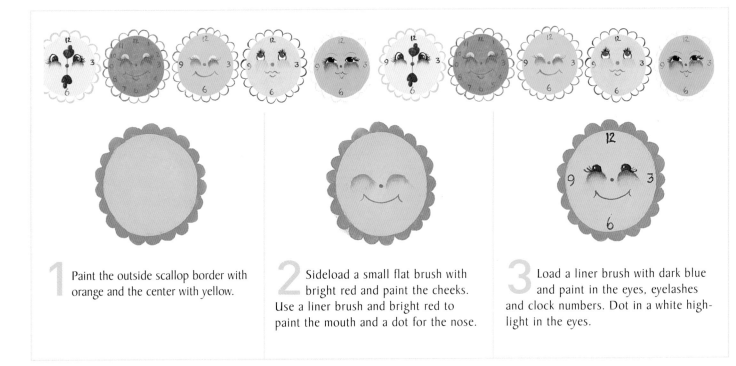

1 Paint the outside scallop border with orange and the center with yellow.

2 Sideload a small flat brush with bright red and paint the cheeks. Use a liner brush and bright red to paint the mouth and a dot for the nose.

3 Load a liner brush with dark blue and paint in the eyes, eyelashes and clock numbers. Dot in a white highlight in the eyes.

Kids

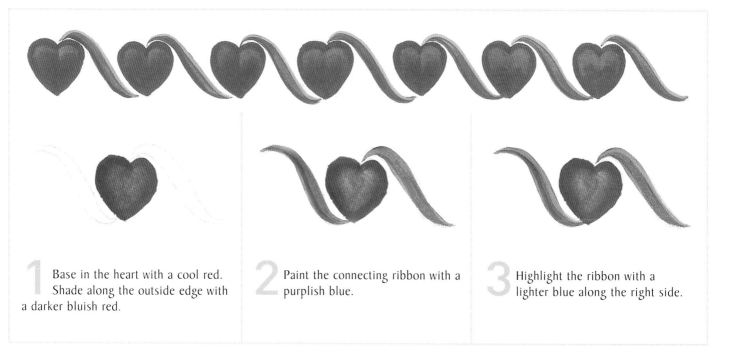

1 Base in the heart with a cool red. Shade along the outside edge with a darker bluish red.

2 Paint the connecting ribbon with a purplish blue.

3 Highlight the ribbon with a lighter blue along the right side.

1 Paint the vine and leaves with dark and medium values of green. Base in the bluebird with a medium blue.

2 Add the wing and tail feathers with white. Dot in a black eye with a tiny white highlight.

3 Finish with a red beak, head feather and little dots on the bird's belly.

Kids

1 Base in the birdhouse, the scallop edge, and the birds with a dark gray-blue.

2 Paint yellow flowers on the house and a white scallop line for the eaves. Add the picket fence with white plus a little blue.

3 Paint the roofline and the hole with black. Finish with green grass along the bottom edge.

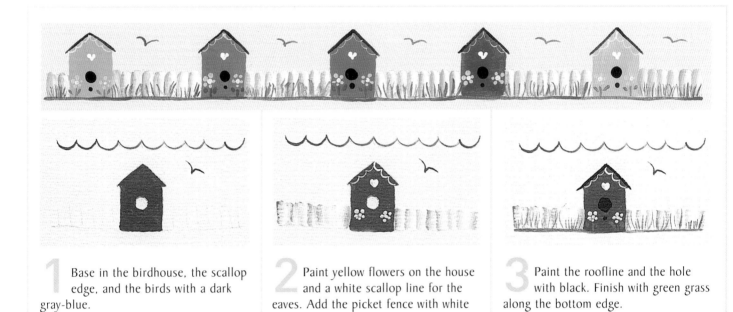

1 Base the goldfish with metallic gold paint. Add the tail fins and side fins with metallic silver.

2 Add the eye and mouth with black on a liner brush.

3 With an aqua blue, paint the waves and a series of four diminishing dots for the bubbles.

Kids

1 Load a round brush with medium blue and paint a fat S-stroke. Shade along the top with dark blue. Lighten the lower edge with medium blue plus white.

2 With white, paint 3 small comma strokes for the tail feathers and wing feathers. Tap very tiny white dots on the chest area.

3 Add the beak with brown and dot in the eye with dark blue. Load a round brush with dark green and paint the leaf shapes on either side.

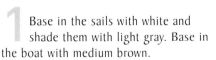

1 Base in the sails with white and shade them with light gray. Base in the boat with medium brown.

2 Paint the top of the mast brown and add very fine black lines along the side of the boat. Add blue, red and yellow stripes on the sails and a red flag at the top.

3 With a brush mix of white and blue, paint the waves.

MARCHING FLOWERS

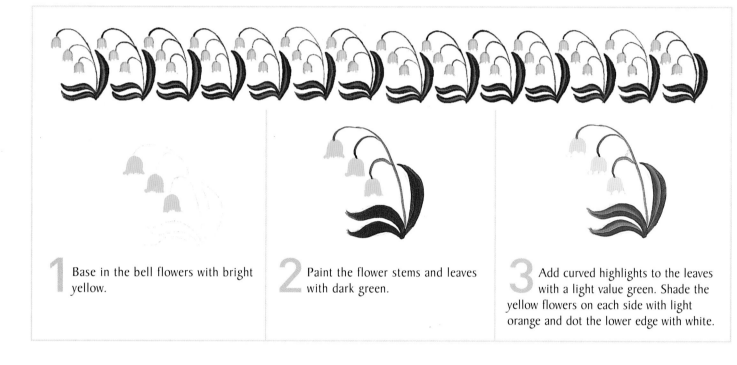

1 Base in the bell flowers with bright yellow.

2 Paint the flower stems and leaves with dark green.

3 Add curved highlights to the leaves with a light value green. Shade the yellow flowers on each side with light orange and dot the lower edge with white.

1 Paint the tulip petals with bright red and shade them with darker red.

2 Paint in the stem and leaves with medium green and shade them with darker green.

3 Finish with little bright red hearts next to the leaves and two dots over the tulip petals.

Marching Flowers

1 With sage green, stroke in the stem, then two long scrolls on either side and two hook strokes. Paint the leaves with a brush mix of sage green and white.

2 Make a brush mix of deep coral pink plus white and paint the daisy petals. Thin the coral and paint the scalloped edge along the bottom.

3 Add the daisy center with ochre and dot in a white highlight to the right of center.

1 Paint the connecting linework, hooks, scrolls and comma strokes with dark green.

2 Load a brush mix of dark blue and white on a liner brush and paint the aster petals.

3 Add a dark blue dot to the center of the flower and white dots in between the scrolls.

CHRISTMAS

1 Base in the snowman with white and the holly sprig with green.

2 Shade the snowman sections with light gray and add black dots for the buttons and face. Vary their size and placement for different expressions.

3 Add a bright red scarf to the snowman and red berries on the holly.

1 Base the tree with medium green and the trunk with brown. Stipple the wreath with dark green.

2 Shade the left side of the tree with darker green and highlight the right side of the tree and the wreath with light green.

3 Add a dark green connecting line and light green strokes above and below. Add the same strokes to the sides of the tree. Finish with red dots and a bow on the wreath.

CHRISTMAS

1 Base in the bright red coat, the brown bag, the black glove, and the tree and trunk with dark green and brown. Base in the facial area with a flesh tone.

2 Shade the bag with a darker brown. Shade the red coat and indicate the sleeve with dark red.

3 Add white trim around the bottom of the coat, the cuff of the sleeve, and the hood. Finish with a white pom-pom at the back of the hood.

1 Paint the angel's coat with medium blue, and the dress, head and hands with ivory. Add four-point stars with a metallic gold.

2 Shade the blue coat with a darker blue along the outside edges and to separate the sleeves from the body.

3 Add three white trim lines at the dress bottom, and red rick-rack trim on the sleeves and coat bottom. Dot the star points with ivory.

Traditional Gold Borders

1 With metallic gold paint on a liner brush, paint elongated C-strokes to make the spine of the border.

2 Add little tulip-and-dot shapes in the V of the spine. If you want other colors besides the gold, paint the tulips pink, as shown in the border at the top.

3 Finish with the little two-stroke leaves above and below the spine. I painted the leaves green to add even more color, as shown at the top.

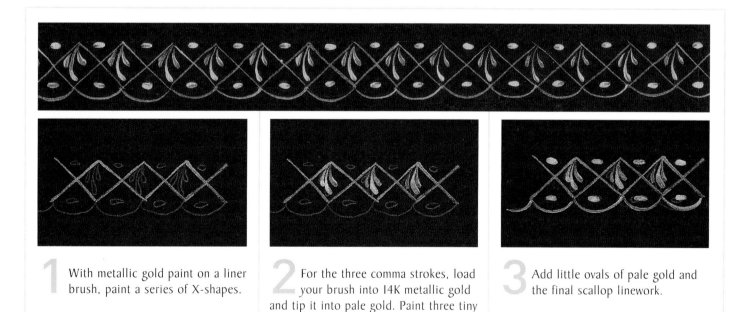

1 With metallic gold paint on a liner brush, paint a series of X-shapes.

2 For the three comma strokes, load your brush into 14K metallic gold and tip it into pale gold. Paint three tiny descending commas.

3 Add little ovals of pale gold and the final scallop linework.

Traditional Gold Borders

1 Load a liner brush with 14K metallic gold paint. Start with the C-stroke spine.

2 Load a round brush in 14K gold, then tip it into pale gold. Paint four commas of decreasing size, starting at the tips and pulling toward the base.

3 Add the scrolls on the top of the C-stroke spine with pale gold on a liner brush.

1 With 14K metallic gold on a liner brush, start with the upper row of cross-over scallops and the lower row of mini scallops.

2 Add the three little comma strokes in the area between the scallops.

3 Finish with crosshatching in the fan-shaped areas of the upper scallops. Add dots above. Below the comma strokes, add a triangle of three dots.

Maple Leaf Swag

1 Base in all the leaf shapes with a light value green on a round brush. Add texture strokes with medium green.

2 With dark green on a small round brush, pull feather strokes from the base of each leaf to represent veins and texture.

3 With light green, pull highlights from the outside edges of the leaves in toward the bases.

4 Add the connecting linework and comma strokes with dark green on a liner brush. Finish with a large dot of dark green at the base of the central leaf.

400 Borders You Can Paint

On the following pages is a wide variety of borders and embellishments you may use to enhance your own painted projects. Copy them as they are, or adapt the size, colors and backgrounds to suit your own tastes. Once you see how easy these are to paint, you can have a lot of fun creating your own borders!

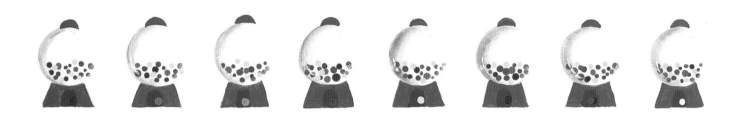

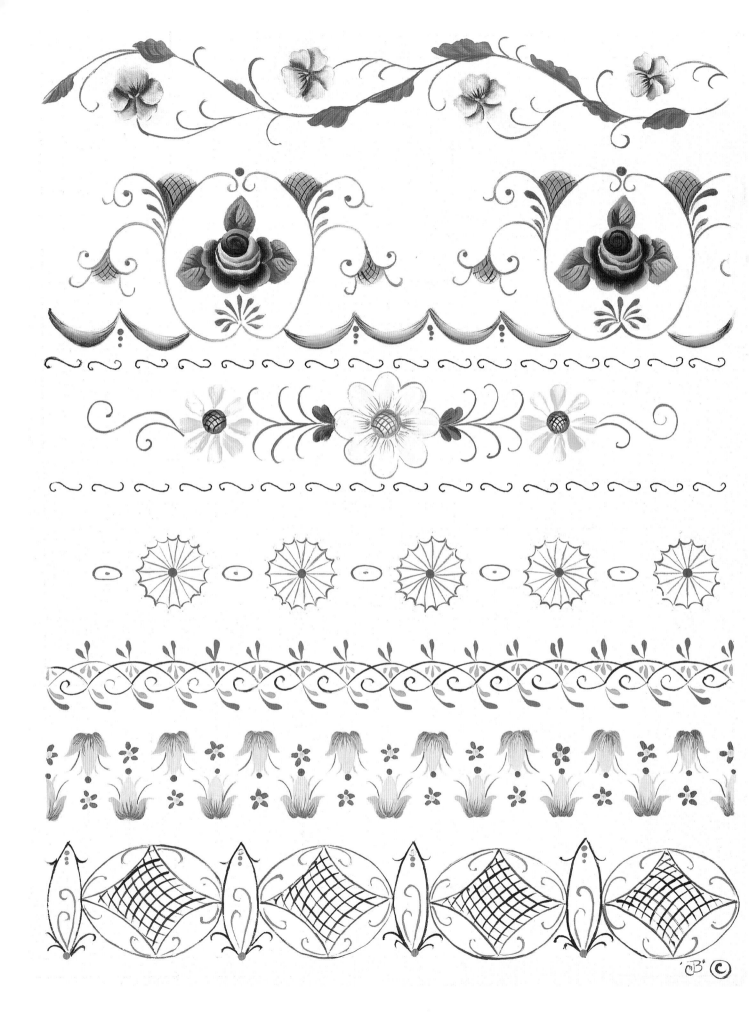

'B' ©

ANNO

B©

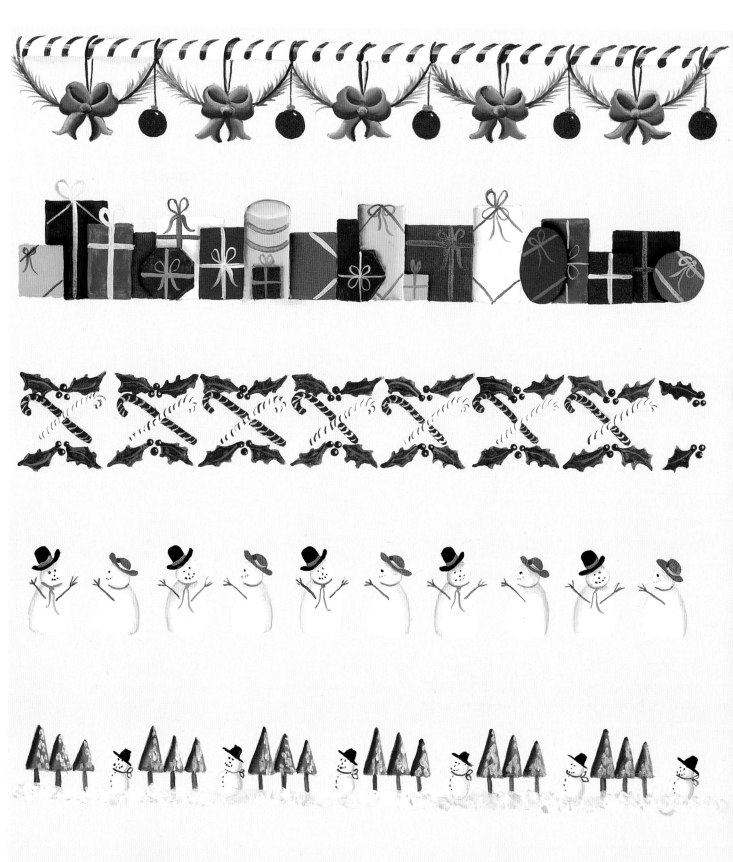

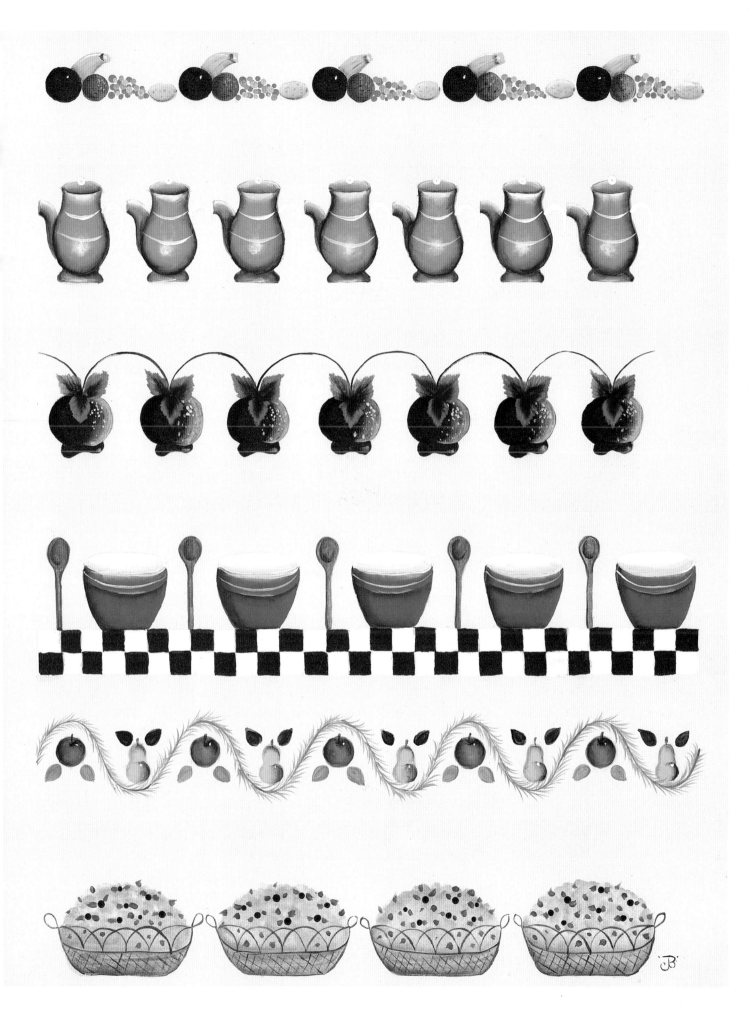

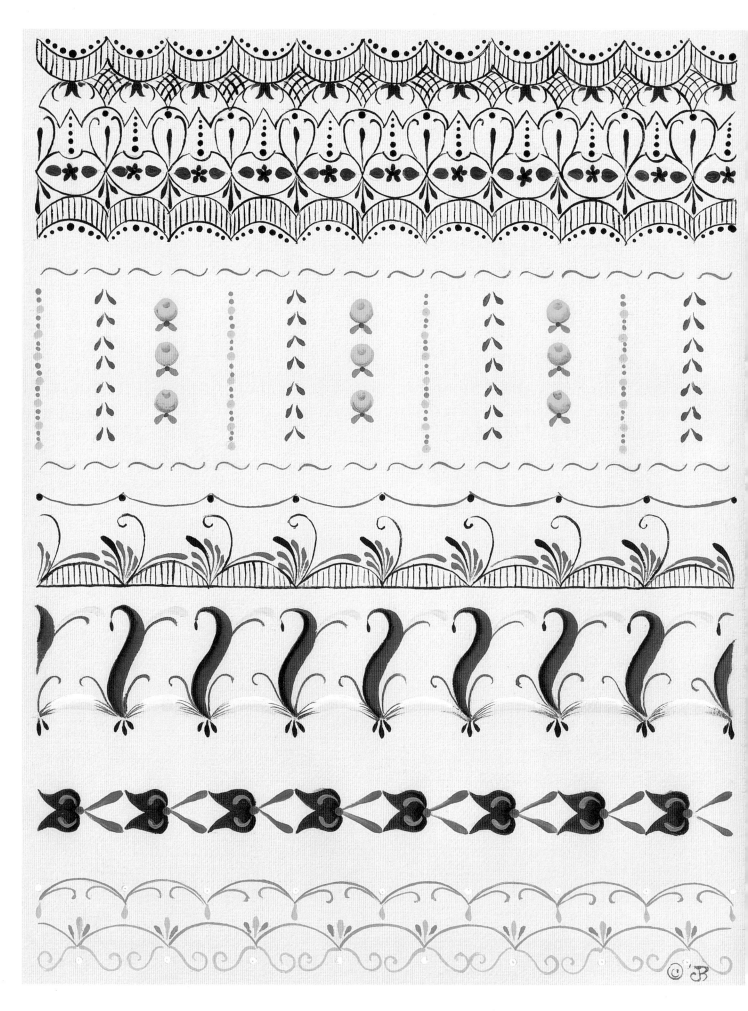

114

117

119

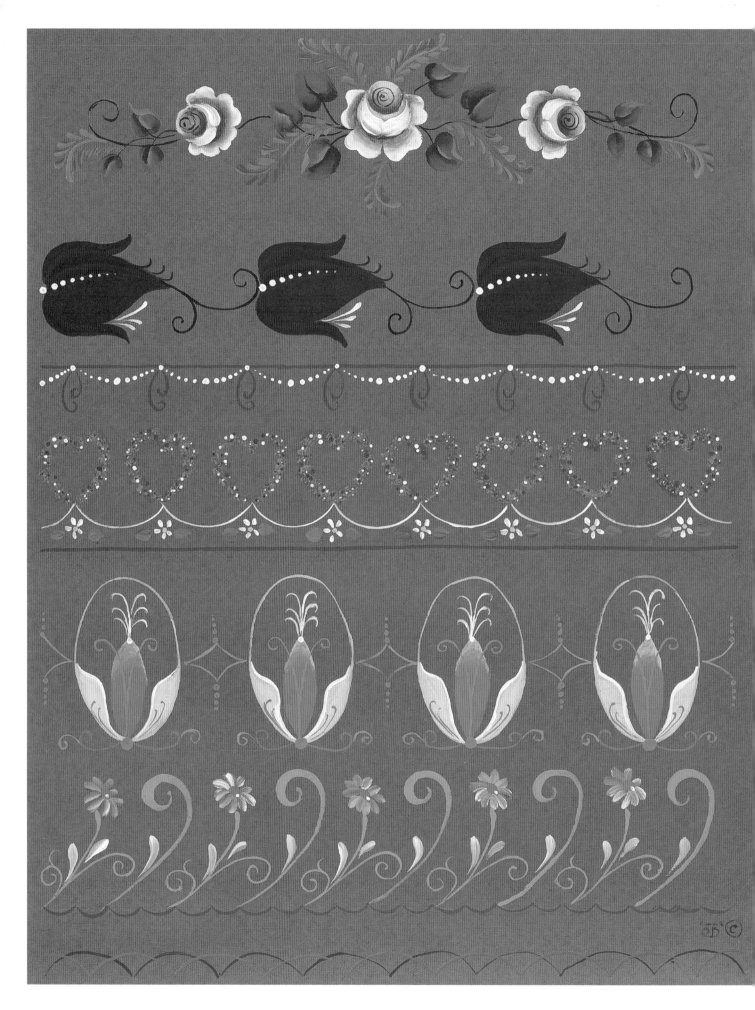

124

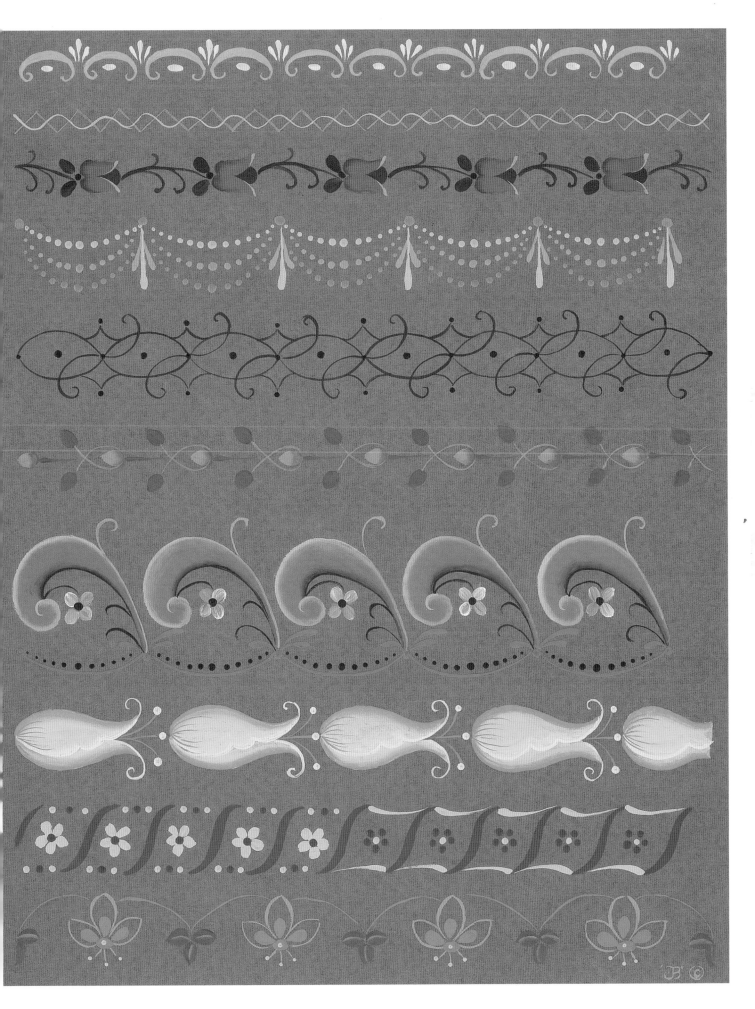

126

127

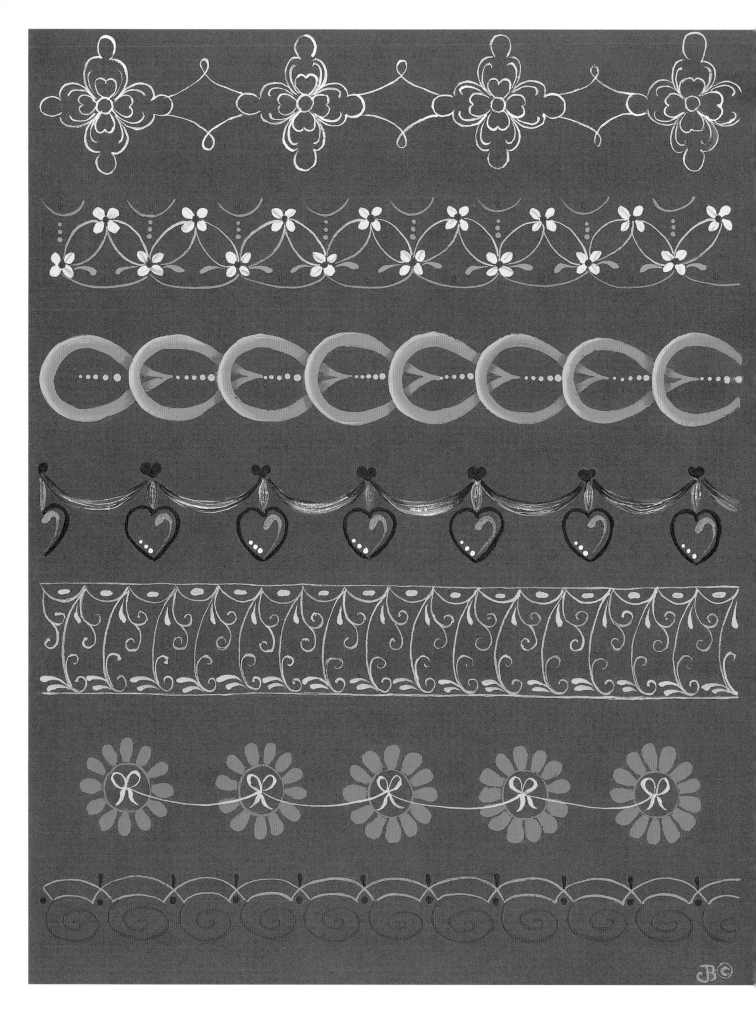

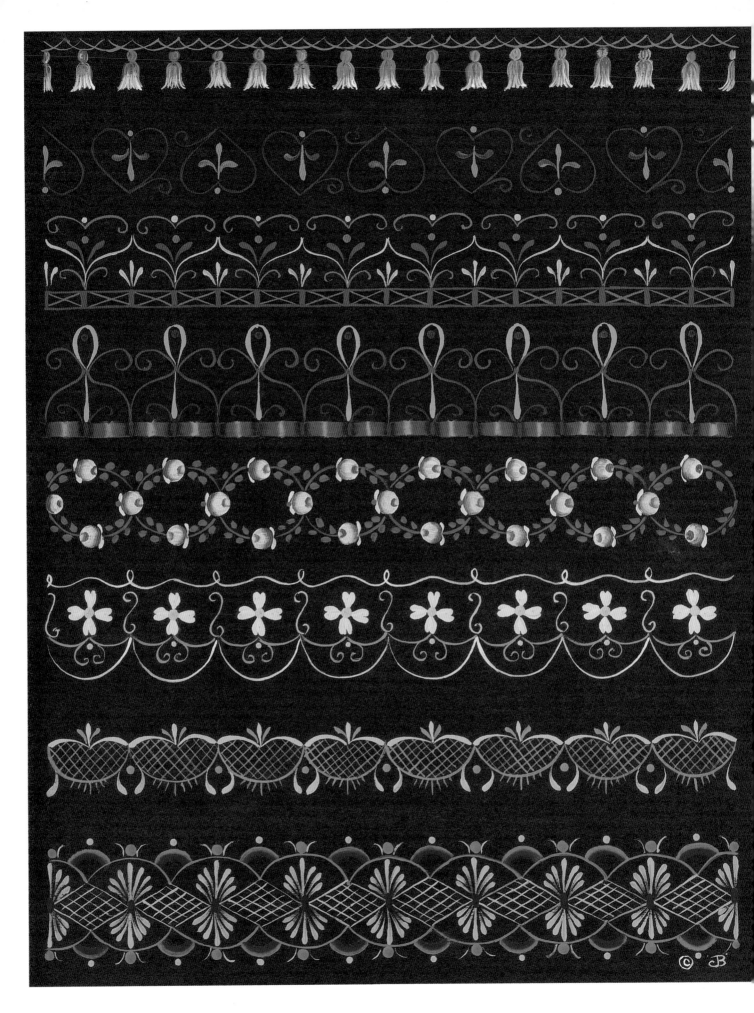

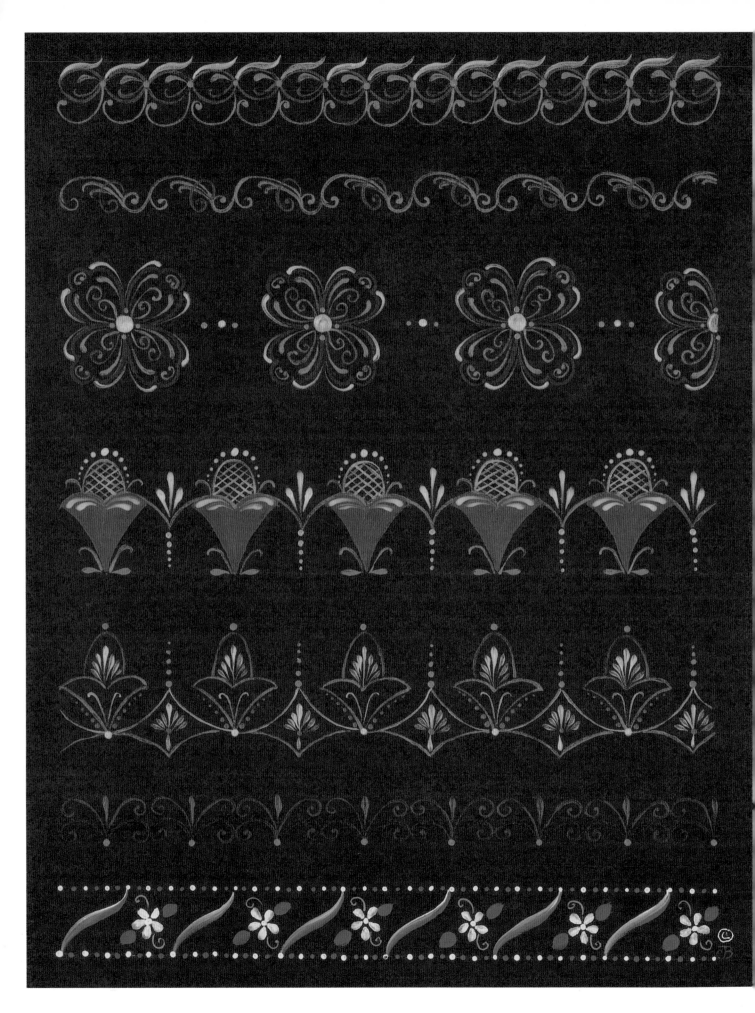

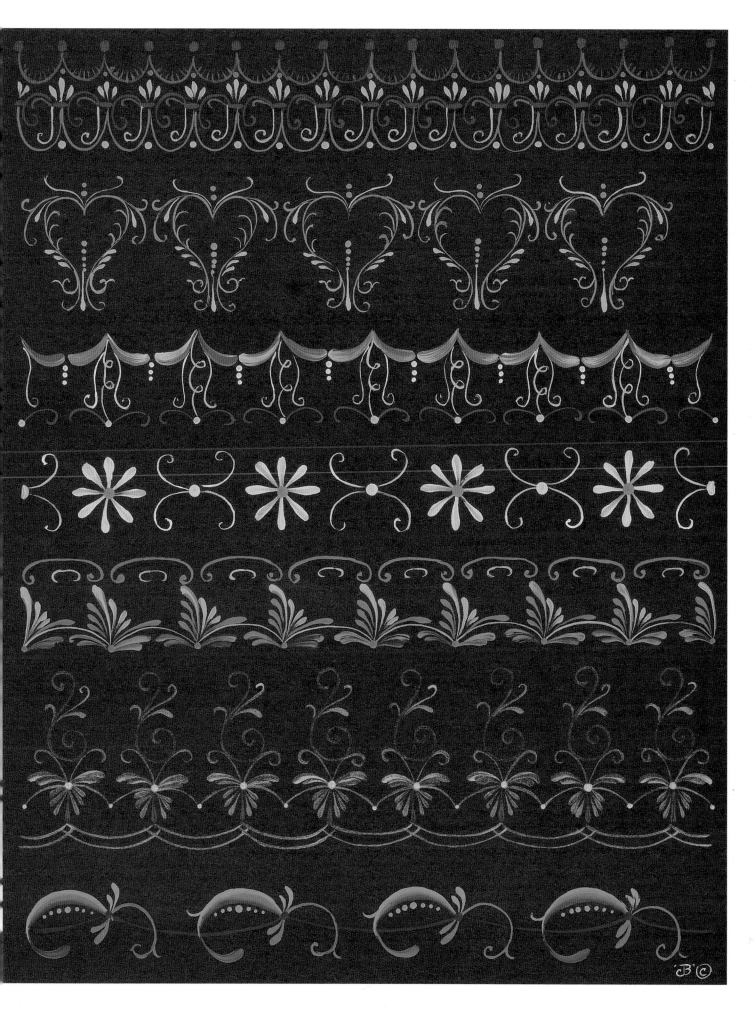

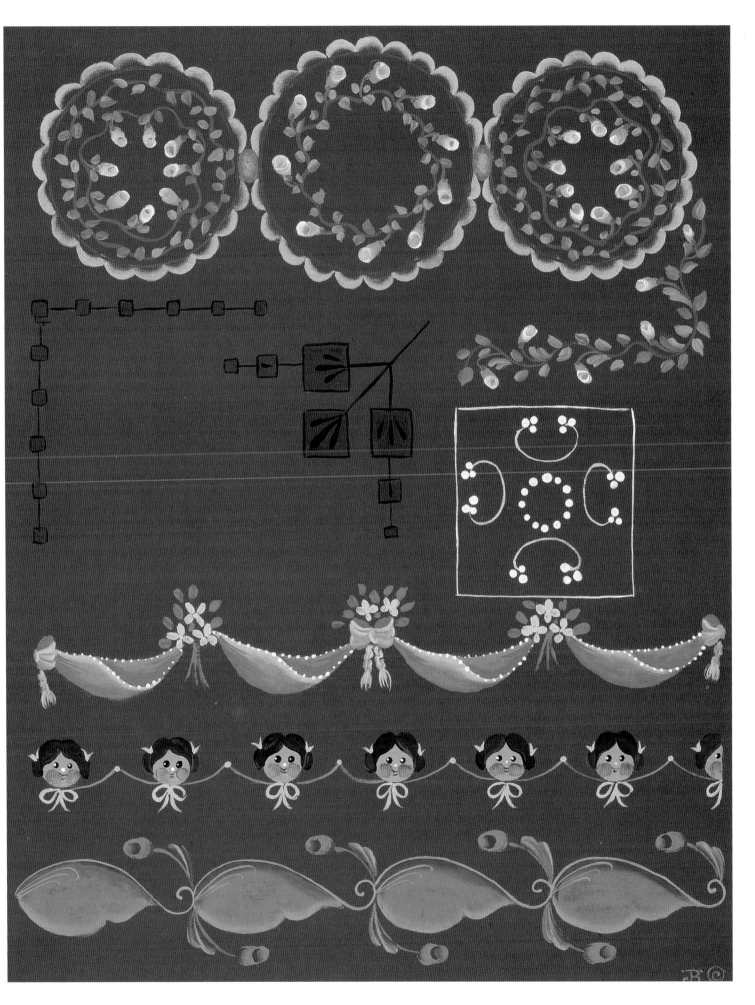

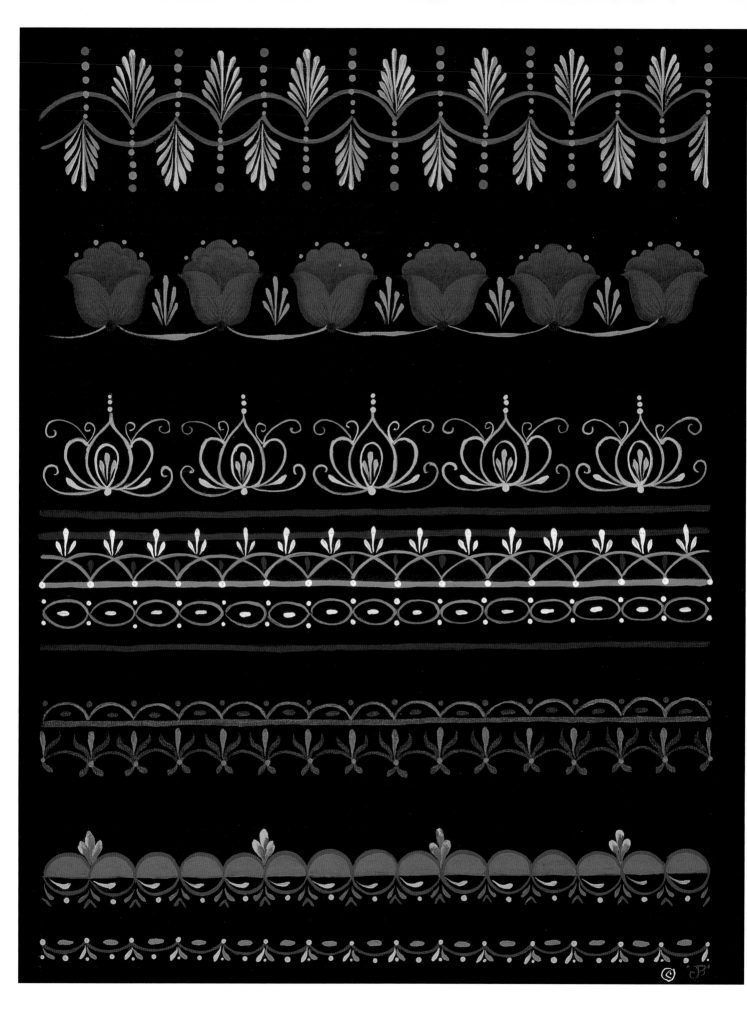

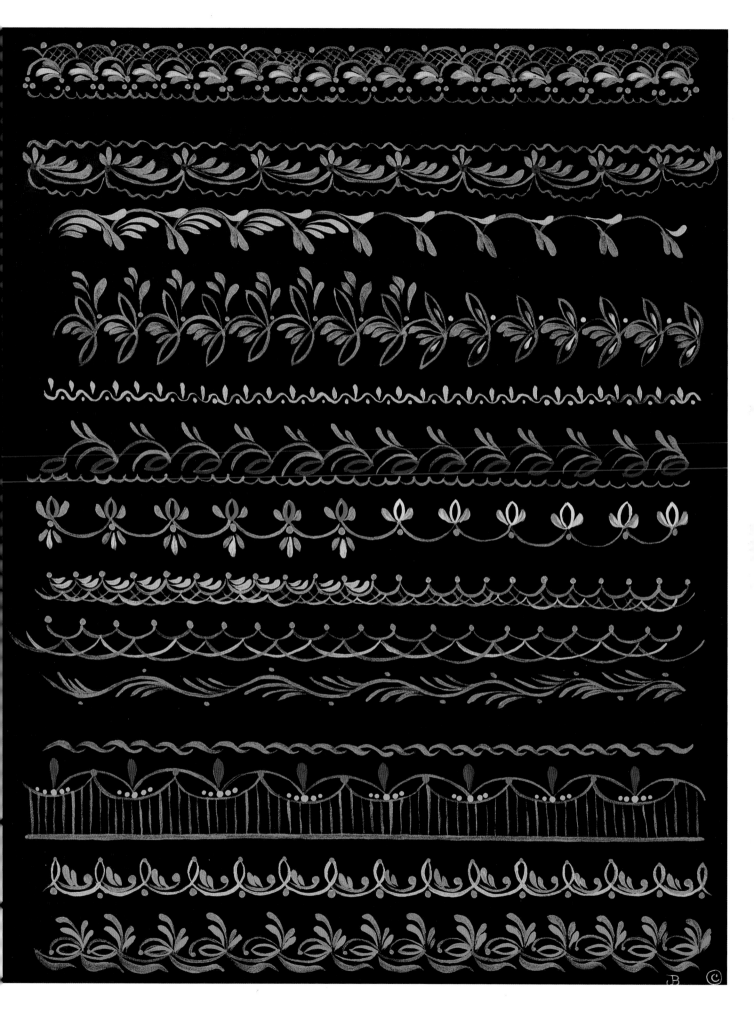

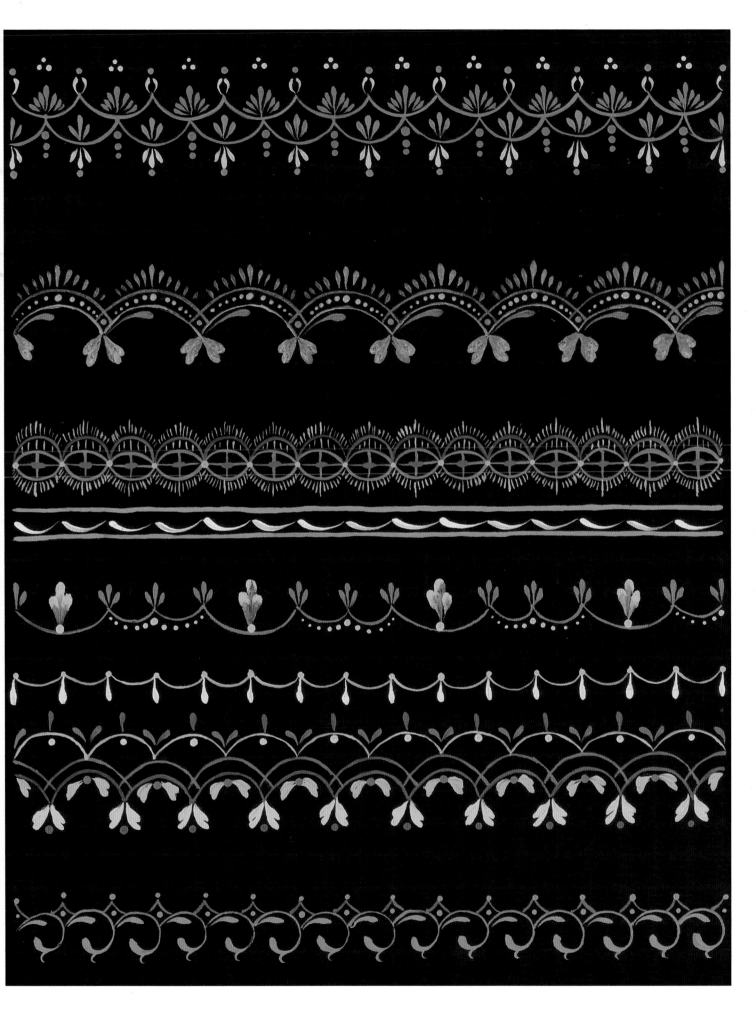

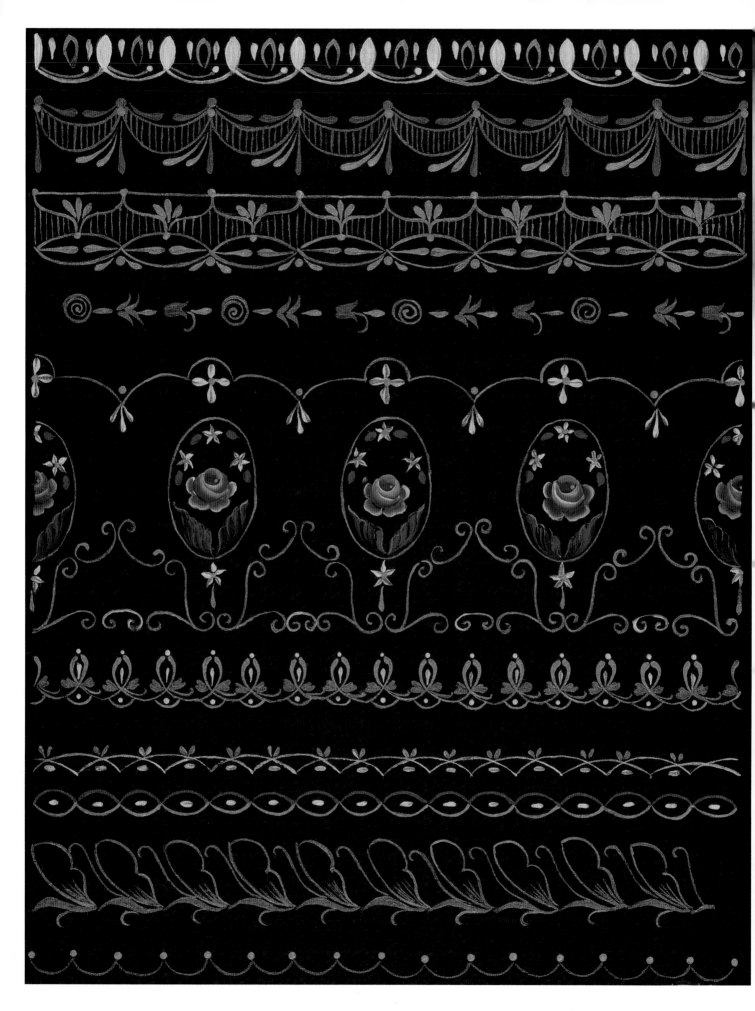

Resources

Jodie Bushman
Rainshadow Studio
P.O. Box 510
Welches, OR 97067
(503) 622-4734

Paints

Delta Ceramcoat Acrylics
Delta Technical Coatings, Inc.
2550 Pellissier Place
Whittier, CA 90601
(800) 423-4135
(562) 695-7969
Fax (562) 695-5805
www.deltacrafts.com

Brushes

Loew-Cornell
563 Chestnut Ave.
Teaneck, NJ 07666
(201) 836-7070
Fax (210) 836-8110
www.loew-cornell.com

Surfaces

Stan Brown Arts & Crafts
13435 N.E. Whitaker Way
Portland, OR 97230
(503) 257-0559
(800) 547-5531
www.stanbrownartsandcrafts.com

Paul Loftness
32443 651st Avenue
Gibbon, MN 55335
(507) 834-6948

Index

Explore the world of decorative painting with North Light Books

The Complete Book of Decorative Painting

This book is the must-have one-stop reference for decorative painters, crafters, home decorators and do-it-yourselfers. It's packed with solutions to every painting challenge, including surface preparation, lettering, faux finishes, strokework techniques and more! You'll also find five fun-to-paint projects designed to instruct, challenge and entertain you—no matter what your skill level.

ISBN 1-58180-062-2, paperback, 256 pages, #31803-K

Decorative Mini-Murals You Can Paint

Add drama to any room in your home with one of these 11 delightful mini-murals! They're perfect for when you don't have the time or the experience to tackle a whole wall. You'll learn which colors and brushes to use, plus you'll find tips and mini-demos for getting the realistic trompe l'oeil effects you love. Includes detailed templates, photos and step-by-step instructions.

ISBN 1-58180-145-9, paperback, 144 pages, #31891-K

Pretty Painted Furniture

Add beauty and elegance to every room in your home! Diane Trierweiler shows you how with step-by-step instructions for giving old furniture a facelift and new furniture a personal touch. Twelve lovely projects, complete with helpful color charts and traceable patterns, teach you how to paint everything from berries to butterflies on chests, chairs, tables and more.

ISBN 1-58180-234-X, paperback, 128 pages, #32009-K

How to Design Your Own Painting Projects

Let Michelle Temares show you the seven easy steps to great design! You'll see how to find ideas and inspiration, develop new designs, create good compositions, and paint your own original designs. "Good" and "bad" examples illustrate each important lesson, while three step-by-step decorative painting projects help you make the leap from initial idea to completed painting.

ISBN 1-58180-263-3, paperback, 128 pages, #32128-K

These books and other fine North Light titles are available from your local art & craft retailer, bookstore, online supplier or by calling 1-800-448-0915.